ANDREW WILSON

1 CORINTHIANS FOR YOU

thegoodbook
COMPANY

1 Corinthians For You

© Andrew Wilson, 2021

Published by:
The Good Book Company

thegoodbook.com | www.thegoodbook.co.uk
thegoodbook.com.au | thegoodbook.co.nz | thegoodbook.co.in

Published in association with the literary agency of Wolgemuth & Associates.

ISBN: 9781784986230

Cover design by Ben Woodcraft | Printed in India

CONTENTS

Series Preface 5

Introduction 7

1. A Surprising Start *1 Corinthians 1:1-31* 11

2. Spirituality and Community *1 Corinthians 2:1 – 3:23* 25

3. Discipline in Theory and in Practice *1 Corinthians 4:1 – 5:13* 39

4. Sex and the City *1 Corinthians 6:1-20* 55

5. Marriage and Singleness *1 Corinthians 7:1-40* 71

6. Laying Down Your Rights *1 Corinthians 8:1 – 9:27* 87

7. The Trouble with Idolatry *1 Corinthians 10:1 – 11:1* 101

8. Covered Heads and Broken Bread *1 Corinthians 11:2-34* 117

9. Gifts, Lordship and Love *1 Corinthians 12:1 – 13:13* 133

10. Eagerly Desire Spiritual Gifts *1 Corinthians 14:1-40* 149

11. Christ Has Been Raised *1 Corinthians 15:1-49* 165

12. A Triumphant Ending *1 Corinthians 15:50 – 16:24* 179

Glossary 195

Bibliography 203

SERIES PREFACE

Each volume of the *God's Word For You* series takes you to the heart of a book of the Bible, and applies its truths to your heart.

The central aim of each title is to be:

- Bible centered
- Christ glorifying
- Relevantly applied
- Easily readable

You can use *1 Corinthians For You:*

To read. You can simply read from cover to cover, as a book that explains and explores the themes, encouragements and challenges of this part of Scripture.

To feed. You can work through this book as part of your own personal regular devotions, or use it alongside a sermon or Bible-study series at your church. Each chapter is divided into two (or occasionally three) shorter sections, with questions for reflection at the end of each.

To lead. You can use this as a resource to help you teach God's word to others, both in small-group and whole-church settings. You'll find tricky verses or concepts explained using ordinary language, and helpful themes and illustrations along with suggested applications.

These books are not commentaries. They assume no understanding of the original Bible languages, nor a high level of biblical knowledge. Verse references are marked in **bold** so that you can refer to them easily. Any words that are used rarely or differently in everyday language outside the church are marked in grey when they first appear, and are explained in a glossary toward the back. There, you'll also find details of resources you can use alongside this one, in both personal and church life.

Our prayer is that as you read, you'll be struck not by the contents of this book, but by the book it's helping you open up; and that you'll praise not the author of this book, but the One he is pointing you to.

Carl Laferton, Series Editor

Bible translations used:

- NIV: New International Version, 2011 edition (this is the version being quoted unless otherwise stated)

- ESV: English Standard Version

- NKJV: New King James Version

INTRODUCTION TO 1 CORINTHIANS

When asked for their favourite Pauline letter, most people take Romans or Ephesians to the ball. My heart will always be with Corinth.

The breadth and scope of 1 Corinthians are breathtaking. It is the most wide-ranging and complete letter Paul wrote; readers who are used to Paul taking several chapters of careful argument to make one or two points—like *Gentiles* * *and Jews should eat together* (Galatians) or even *thanks for the gift* (Philippians)—will be amazed at the sheer variety of subjects that Paul tackles and the punchy clarity with which he speaks.

My affection for this letter is inspired by several aspects of it. Partly it is because it summarises the central themes of the Christian faith so crisply and beautifully. The cross: "We preach Christ crucified" (1:23). Grace: "What do you have that you did not receive?" (4:7). God: "There is one God, the Father, from whom all things came and for whom we live; and there is but one Lord, Jesus Christ" (8:6). Mission: "I have become all things to all people so that by all possible means I might save some" (9:22). Love: "So now faith, hope, and love abide, these three; but the greatest of these is love" (13:13, ESV). The gospel: "… that Christ died for our sins in accordance with the Scriptures, that he was buried, that he was raised on the third day in accordance with the Scriptures" (15:3-4, ESV). Hope: "The last enemy to be destroyed is death" (15:26). It is a pithy, profound and quotable epistle.

Partly it is because I love corporate worship. Without 1 Corinthians it would be hard to imagine how church services actually worked in the New Testament. We would know next to nothing about the Lord's Supper in these first-generation churches. We would have no idea how spiritual gifts are supposed to function in Christian worship. Thanks to the chaos in Corinth and Paul's response to it, we have plenty of guidance on both counts.

---

* Words in grey are defined in the Glossary (page 195).

Partly it is because I am a pastor in a large, cosmopolitan and very diverse city. The people in my community, like the people in Corinth, worship lots of different gods and have sex with lots of different people. This letter helps me think through how to help them, with specifics on practical application—sexuality, idolatry, food, divorce, remarriage, singleness, adultery, church discipline and even incest—that I would not find anywhere else.

> It is vital that we think and talk about grace, but sometimes we just need to *see* grace.

And partly it is because the Corinthians were a mess, and God loved them anyway. It is vital that we think about grace, and talk about grace, but sometimes we just need to *see* grace. Sometimes we need to watch an exasperated apostle talking to a rebellious and divisive church with tenderness and affection and with a faith that believes in the transformation that can only come from the power of the Spirit, the example of Christ and the faithfulness of God. That's what this letter puts so richly on display. It brings hope to "Corinthians" everywhere, including me.

Welcome to Corinth

Roman Corinth was a large, bustling, commercial and pluralistic city in southern Greece. It was the regional capital of Achaia, known among other things for its port on the Peloponnesian isthmus, its sexual promiscuity, and its hosting of the biennial Isthmian Games. Originally a Greek city, it had been destroyed by the Romans in 146 BC and then rebuilt by Julius Caesar a hundred years later. We cannot be sure how large it was in Paul's day—I have seen figures ranging from a population of 20,000 to 800,000!—but an estimate of between 40,000 and 60,000 is probably about right (see Rinse Willet, "Whirlwind of

Numbers: Demographic Experiments for Roman Corinth" in *Ancient Society* 42 (2012), pages 127-158).

Paul had founded the church on his second missionary journey, spending a year and a half there after hearing in a dream that God had many people in the city (Acts 18:1-11). This letter was written a few years later, in the spring of AD 54 or 55, in response to receiving a worrying letter (see 1 Corinthians 7:1) and some even more worrying news (1:11) from the members of the church. As with the city, it is hard to be sure how large the church was. It cannot have been much fewer than 50, given all the names and households Paul mentions. But it is unlikely to have been more than 200 because the whole church met together in one place, whether in Gaius's house (Romans 16:23) or another venue like a restaurant or barn (see Edward Adams, *The Earliest Christian Meeting Places: Almost Exclusively Houses?*). If we imagine a church of 100 in a city of 50,000, we will not be too far out. It might encourage us to realise how similar those numbers are to the situation of many churches today—and it might also help us understand how outnumbered the Christians were and what implications that had for the life of the church.

We need to understand this because the most striking thing about the Corinthian church was not its size or its demographic makeup, but the degree to which worldly ideas and practices were accepted in the congregation. It is as if the boundaries between the church and the world had almost disappeared. Some New Testament churches struggled with opposition and persecution from the cities around them. The Corinthians faced the opposite problem: assimilation into a pagan, promiscuous, competitive and idolatrous culture. Much of Paul's effort in writing this letter—whether it relates to leadership, sexuality, the nature of the church, idol food, corporate worship or the resurrection—aims to re-establish the differences between the church and the city, and between Christianity and idolatry. That is one of many reasons why it is such a helpful text for those of us who live in the **post-Christian** West.

Structurally, the letter is very simple. There are five major sections of material, bookended by a short introduction and thanksgiving and a concluding chapter of instructions, travel plans and greetings:

Introduction and thanksgiving (1:1-9)

I.   Divisions and the cross (1:10 – 4:21)

II.   Flee sexual immorality (5:1 – 7:40)

III.   Flee idolatry (8:1 – 11:1)

IV.   Corporate worship (11:2 – 14:40)

V.   The resurrection of the body (15:1-58)

Concluding instructions, travel plans and greetings (16:1-24)

We'll work through these sections, pretty much verse by verse, sometimes using the second part of a chapter to pause and consider in more detail a major theme of that passage.

Let's start.

1. A SURPRISING START

If you or I had written 1 Corinthians, it would have been a lot shorter.

The church at Corinth was in a terrible mess. We will find that out very quickly. This letter gives a host of examples: squabbling, incest, sleeping with prostitutes, idolatry, drunkenness during **Communion**, chaotic worship services, denying the future resurrection, and who knows what else. If I was writing to them, I wouldn't have had the patience for sixteen chapters of careful argument and pastoral wisdom. I would have sent a single paragraph, a theological drone strike with the sole aim of blowing their appalling behaviour off the face of the earth:

Andrew, called to be an apostle by the will of God, and our brother Sosthenes, to the church of God in Corinth: Stop. Now. Repent, apologise, change your ways, and I might find it in my heart to talk to you again next winter. Grace be with you. Amen.

Paul does something very different, and it tells us a lot. The length of the letter and the **rhetorical** care with which it is written reveal how much Paul loves the Corinthians and wants to win them over. The depth of **theological** argument, even when addressing things that you would think are obvious (like "Christians shouldn't have sex with prostitutes"), highlights his desire for believers not just to change their actions but to understand why they should do so. His tender language displays his affection for them. The way he sandwiches his **ethical** teaching between sections on the cross (chapter 1) and the resurrection (chapter 15) shows that for Paul, the gospel really is the beginning and the end of the Christian life.

But it is this opening paragraph in **1:1-9*** that provides the sharp-est contrast between the way I would have written this letter, venting and blustering my way through an angry rant, and the way Paul did. (Sosthenes is mentioned as well in **verse 1**, but he is probably a **scribe** or secretary rather than a co-author, so from now on I will refer to the author as Paul.) A few things leap off the page as we consider the first nine verses.

One is how Jesus-centred they are. The passage almost sounds jar-ring. Jesus Christ is mentioned by name nine times in nine verses: as the one who called Paul to be an apostle (**v 1**), the one in whom the Corinthians have been made holy and upon whose name they call (**v 2**), the giver of grace (**v 3**) and the one in whom that grace has been given (**v 4**). Jesus is the source of all riches (**v 5**), the subject of Paul's preach-ing (**v 6**) and the basis for Christian hope (**v 7**). The whole of history is pointing forward to the day of our Lord Jesus Christ (**v 8**), when he shall return as Judge and King. Yet this same Jesus is the one with whom we have fellowship—communion, life-in-common—in the meantime: "Jesus Christ our Lord" (**v 9**). To Paul, Jesus is everything.

As a result, Paul is deeply grateful for the church in spite of all that he knows about them. Partly this stems from God's call, which (as for every church) is a call to be "holy people" (**v 2**—or "saints", ESV). Partly it flows from his experience of the power of God's grace, which has transformed their lives and thereby backed up the truthfulness of Paul's message, "confirming our testimony about Christ among you" (**v 6**). It is also a result of the spiritual gifts that God has poured out on the church (**v 7**), enriching them in every way and particularly with all speech and knowledge (**v 5**). These gifts have not been handled wisely, and Paul will return to this later. But for now, the fact that God has given so many gifts (*charismata*) to the church is a reason for thankfulness.

Most strikingly, Paul displays an astonishing level of confidence in the Corinthians' future. "He will also keep you firm to the end, so

---

* All 1 Corinthians verse references being looked at in each chapter part are in **bold**.

that you will be blameless on the day of our Lord Jesus Christ" (**v 8**). Firm to the end? Blameless? I can think of New Testament churches to whom I could have written that—the Philippians or the Thessalonians perhaps, but not the Corinthians! Yet Paul is certain. They will be confirmed to the end. They will be irreproachable on the day of judgment. And his basis for saying so is not the moral performance of the church on earth but the absolute faithfulness of God in heaven. God's commitment to his people is the guarantee that the Corinthians will make it, in spite of all the sin that characterises them at the moment (and all the warnings Paul will issue later). The same is true of believers today. "God is faithful" (**v 9**).

An Appeal for Unity

How do you identify the main point of a letter? It is easy with emails because there is a "subject" line at the top. It is easy with texts and WhatsApp messages because they are so short. But it can be harder in other forms of communication, especially when there is a significant cultural distance between the writer/speaker and the reader/hearer.

When my wife, Rachel, was learning how to teach English as a foreign language, she had to learn how to teach someone the basics of a business phone call in English. In many cultures, she discovered, business people state their reason for phoning straight away, as we might in an email. But English people don't speak to people on the phone like that. What they do, explained the teacher, is both very predictable and very odd. They greet one another and talk about nothing of any real importance for up to thirty seconds. Then there will be a pause for about a second, at which point the caller will say either "So…" or "Anyway…" or "The reason I'm calling is…" Only then do you find out what the conversation is actually going to be about. (Think about it: if you're English, I bet you'll discover it's true of you.) Rachel finished the lesson quite baffled—not because this formula wasn't accurate but because it was completely accurate and she had never noticed.

In Paul's world, letters followed a fairly set pattern, much like phone calls do in ours, and you can see it in this chapter. You would identify yourself (**v 1**) and then the people to whom you were writing (**v 2**), greeting them with peace (**v 3**; Paul, as obsessed with the kindness of God as always, adds "grace"). Usually you would give thanks for the other person, whether for their health, their letter, their friendship, or something else (**v 4-9**). With those introductory elements out the way, you would then turn to the reason for your letter. In the case of 1 Corinthians, it is this: "that all of you agree with one another in what you say and that there be no divisions among you, but that you be perfectly united in mind and thought" (**v 10**).

In light of all the issues that will crop up later, unity might not seem like the obvious priority. It might seem as if Paul is easing into the letter, beginning with the low-hanging fruit before turning to genuinely controversial matters. But when you consider the major problems in the church, you notice that almost all of them are characterised by a combination of pride and division. There is pride and division over leaders (chapters 1 – 4), sexual ethics (chapters 5 – 6), litigation (chapter 6), marriage (chapter 7), idol food (chapters 8 – 10), corporate worship (chapter 11), spiritual gifts (chapters 12 – 14) and even the resurrection (chapter 15). Taken in isolation, each issue could be tackled on its own merits. But Paul is a wise pastor. He can see the common thread—division—running through all the problems. So he addresses it up front and gets to the specifics later.

There are quarrels in the church, which Paul knows about because people from Chloe's household have told him (**1:11**). There are factions in the community, each identifying with a different leader: Paul, **Apollos**, Peter (called here by his Aramaic name, Cephas) and Christ (**v 12**). We will never know exactly why the various groups took these different names. I like to think of them as the Spiritual, the Sophisticated, the Serious and the Smug—we clearly have some who regard themselves as more spiritual than everyone else (chapters 2 – 3, 12 – 14), some who love eloquent worldly wisdom and "know" that idols don't really exist (chapters 1, 8 – 10), some who are much more cautious about both of these and would be regarded as "weak" by either or both of the others, and a final group of which all we know is their slogan: "I follow Christ". But my guess is no more likely than anyone else's.

What we do know is that each of these four men would have been appalled to see their names used in such a way. Paul is horrified by it and quickly marshals a flurry of arguments to expose how destructive it is (**1:13**). *Christ is not divided, is he?* says Paul, *so how can the church be? Paul wasn't crucified for you, was he, so how can you possibly put his name alongside that of Jesus? You weren't baptised into the name of Paul, were you? So why would you put loyalty to me ahead of loyalty to the body of Christ?* Paul is responding so quickly that he forgets how many people he has baptised and has to correct himself (**v 14-16**). But he makes this point because he wants to remind the Corinthians that their ultimate allegiance is to Jesus rather than to him. Baptism was never Paul's primary mission. His primary mission was to preach the gospel of the cross of Christ, in which all human self-importance comes to nothing (**v 17**).

Three Types of Foolishness

The primary problem in the church, and Paul's main reason for writing this letter in the first place, is division (**v 10**). But we divide because of pride; the root of factionalism is almost always self-importance and arrogance. So before engaging with the factions and leaders in more detail in chapters 3 and 4, Paul looks first to cut the legs out from underneath worldly divisions by skewering human pride. He does this by drawing a series of contrasts—wise/foolish, strong/weak, influential/lowly—and showing how the gospel puts us on the "wrong" side of all of them. In our preaching, our message and our very existence we are foolish, weak and lowly. So if we are going to blow our trumpets about anything, it had better not be ourselves or any human leaders. Rather, "let the one who boasts boast in the Lord" (**1:31**).

Christian preaching is fundamentally foolish, at least in the eyes of the world. The world, in Paul's day, had all sorts of wonderful techniques to make its messages more acceptable: wisdom, eloquence, intelligence, legal reasoning, philosophy (**v 17-20**). Our generation has added the power of advertising, popular music, newspapers, movies, websites and television shows which push a particular vision of the true, the good or the beautiful, and by presenting it well make it seem more plausible. Meanwhile the church is stuck with a method that looked foolish in ancient Corinth and looks even more foolish now: preaching. Not with tricks or stunts. Not with high-budget special effects or virtual-reality immersive experiences. Not with wisdom or eloquence, "lest the cross of Christ be emptied of its power" (**v 17**). Just proclaiming what God has done in Christ and trusting that God will use that message to turn people's lives the right way up.

Hopefully this is obvious, but this is not an argument for long, dull, rambling, monotone, unimaginative sermons. I have sat through a few of those, and they have nothing to do with Paul's point here. In this very letter, Paul proves himself a master of punchy, witty, direct, well-illustrated, concise, rhetorical, funny and incisive communication (and I spend a good deal of my time trying to communicate like that myself). Instead, it is an argument for recognising where the power to save really comes from: not from the polish, the pranks or the presentation but from the proclamation of Jesus Christ, crucified and risen. As a recruitment strategy in a visually saturated world, it is foolishness. Yet that was how God saved the Corinthians and how he has saved everybody since: "God was pleased through the foolishness of what was preached to save those who believe" (**v 21**). The Corinthian church, in which each member's testimony was that they were saved simply by hearing the message of Christ crucified, was living proof that it works.

It is not just the method that is foolish, though; the message is foolish as well. "Jews demand signs and Greeks look for wisdom, but we preach Christ crucified: a stumbling-block to Jews and foolishness to Gentiles" (**v 22-23**). Jewish people, as we know from the four Gospels, were eager for "signs" that would accompany and authorise the **Messiah**, just like many today look for religious experiences (for instance, Matthew 12:38; 16:1; John 2:18; 4:48). Greek people prized *sophia*, "wisdom", in the same way that modern people might prize reason or science. In that world, Paul says, our message is preposterous: a crucified Messiah looks like a complete contradiction to Jews and utter lunacy to everyone else. Yet when this crazy message is heard by people whom God has called, whether they are Jews or Gentiles, it turns out to be both God's power and his wisdom (1 Corinthians **1:24**). The most apparently ridiculous thing that God has ever done is, it turns out, far smarter than the cleverest thing that human beings have ever come up with (**v 25**).

> A crucified Messiah looks like a contradiction to Jews and lunacy to everyone else.

Having shown the foolishness of Christian preaching and the Christian message, Paul moves to his masterful punchline: the Corinthian church's very existence is foolish. *Look at yourselves*, he says. *When you became believers, you weren't a high-powered, rich, upmarket group of movers and shakers* (v 26). *But God saved you anyway. He took hold of the weak, the shameful, the vulnerable, the poor and the poorly educated, and turned them— you!—into demonstrations of his transforming favour.* (The Corinthian church, like most revivals in church history, was mainly drawn from among the poor.) *The fact that this church exists at all is proof that God chooses foolish things over wise things, so that nobody might boast before him* (v 27-29). *You are not wise, righteous, holy and redeemed because of your backgrounds,* Paul points out to them, *but because you are "in Christ Jesus" (**v 30**). You were foolish people who heard a foolish message preached in a foolish way—and God has demonstrated his wisdom in you so powerfully that the smartest people on earth are left scratching their heads and wondering how he did it. So if you're going to boast about anything, you should boast in the Lord (**v 31**).*

Questions for reflection

1. Which are you more aware of in your church: the flaws that need correction or the evidences of God's grace? How does Paul's introduction help you with this?

2. What secondary issues or individual loyalties make you most tempted to divide from other Christians?

3. In what ways do people today regard Christianity as foolish? How is this different from the way it was regarded in Paul's day? Why?

PART TWO

The Power of the Cross

"But God chose the foolish things of the world to shame the
wise; God chose the weak things of the world to shame the
strong." (1:27)

The ways of the world have only been turned upside down once, and
that was at Calvary.

A Christian would say that, of course. The cross is our central symbol. It is the way in which people are forgiven from sin and reconciled
to God, the place where we see the love of God made known to us,
and the focal point of our worship, our prayers, our preaching and our
common meal. In this very letter, Paul spells out for us what is "of first
importance" in the Christian faith: "that Christ died for our sins according to the Scriptures, that he was buried, that he was raised on the third
day according to the Scriptures, and that he appeared to Cephas, and
then to the Twelve [apostles]" (15:3-5). So it is no surprise that disciples
of Jesus would regard the death and resurrection of Jesus as the most
significant, transformative thing that has ever happened.

But the cross did not just change everything for Christians. It began
a process of transformation that has spread to every nation on earth,
and that has affected the way we understand what it is to be human,
what we owe to our fellow citizens, what love looks like, and how we
should treat those who are weak, vulnerable or oppressed. All across
the world, and particularly in those countries where Christianity has
been influential for a long time, ethical frameworks are shaped by the
cross. Whether we are Christians or not, our sense of right and wrong
has been changed for ever by Christ crucified.

There are all sorts of things that we assume to be true—to the
extent that we have enshrined them in our laws, our tax systems, our
international agreements and organisations, and so on—which most
people in the ancient Roman world would either have assumed to be
false, or never even thought about. We assume, for example, that rich

people ought to pay taxes to ensure that poor people have enough to eat, somewhere to sleep, medical care and a safety net for their children. We are deeply concerned about the suffering of vulnerable people in countries we have never visited, often to the point of giving money and time to send relief to them. We oppose torture. We abhor slavery. Sex-selective abortion or infanticide appals us. We believe that a person does not need to be part of our tribe or nation to qualify for our sympathy and support; they simply need to share our humanity. Humility is more attractive to us than boastfulness. We take it as read that all people are created equal, and if someone was to say that they weren't, then we would dismiss them as part of the lunatic fringe. Convictions like this seem incredibly obvious to us, and they stand behind our notion of human rights, our environmental responsibilities, the way we think about military conflict and pretty much all of the ethical questions we face.

Yet none of those things would have been remotely obvious to an ancient Greek or Roman (unless they happened to be Jewish). Infanticide was commonplace in the ancient world. Generals would happily boast of the hundreds of thousands of people they had killed. The fact that migrants from Asia or Africa were drowning in the Mediterranean would not have bothered them in the slightest. Giving to the poor, when it happened, was done in order to gain a reputation; it would have been near unthinkable for it to be done secretly, let alone legally required.

Slavery was universal and unchallenged. When the Roman writer Pliny wanted to find out information about the early Christian movement, he very matter-of-factly told Emperor Trajan that he had tortured two slave women to find out about it, but they hadn't really helped that much (and there is no suggestion that either Pliny or the emperor considered this at all immoral or wicked). We watch people pretend to be killed on TV; they watched people actually being killed in the arena and thought nothing of it. Most of us oppose the death penalty, and if we don't, we would insist that it be done as humanely, painlessly and privately as possible; they crucified people in public and left victims hanging there for days. We think it self-evident that all people are created equal. They thought it self-evident that all people were not. We could go on.

The massive difference between these two worlds is remarkable. I remember thinking about it a lot when I visited Rome. You can walk for three miles, virtually in a straight line, from the Colosseum at one end of the city to the Vatican at the other, past the Roman Forum, through the Centro Storico, over the Tiber, and finally across the Piazza San Pietro into St Peter's Basilica. At the start of your walk, you are standing outside a building in which Christians were literally torn to pieces by wild animals, while tens of thousands of people watched and cheered. At the end, you are standing in a church building of almost inconceivable grandeur and beauty, looking at Michelangelo's Pietà, a statue of Mary holding the dead body of Jesus. The shock is not that the visuals at either end of the city centre form such a contrast; that happens in lots of places. It is that the values, the moral frameworks and the concepts of what it is to be human and how we should treat one another are as utterly different from each other as you could imagine. And the reason for the difference—the historical explanation for the bizarre contrast between the Rome of the Colosseum and the Rome of the Vatican—is the figure that Michelangelo's Mary is cradling in her arms: the crucified Christ.

(Two quick sidenotes here, since I'm talking about the Pietà. (1) As artistically stunning and historically fascinating as it is, I think that making statues of Jesus is a very bad idea, and at least part of what God was banning in the second commandment. (2) There were plenty of abuses in fifteenth-century Roman Catholicism as well—it wasn't all sumptuous paintings and Renaissance statues—so we should admit that the Vatican's behaviour did not always live up to the Christlike values of its art. (3) Michelangelo sculpted it when he was 22. If that doesn't make you feel like an underachiever, nothing will.)

The cross presents us with the most extraordinary inversion in history. It pits the epitome of weakness against the epitome of strength, and weakness wins. It takes a bleeding, naked, brutalised and dying victim and puts him next to the military and legal might of the most powerful, wealthy and unstoppable empire the world had yet known. The contrast continues in the next generations: the power of Emperors Caligula, Claudius, Nero and Domitian against this tiny sect of Messianic Jewish oddballs proclaiming that Jesus rather than Caesar was Lord (as Paul does in this letter), and often being imprisoned or executed for it.

Yet 2,000 years later, it is very obvious that the weak things of the world have shamed the strong and that divine foolishness is wiser than human wisdom. Our moral imagination is that of the Pieta, not the arena. The cross—a stark symbol that was supposed to mean *Roma Victor*—has come to mean *Christus Victor*. Those the ancient world regarded as heroes have become villains, and the crucified criminal has become the most admired and worshipped figure in history. As the classicist T.R. Glover once mischievously put it, we now call our dogs Nero and our sons Paul.

> The story of how the crucifixion turned our ethical framework upside down (or right-side up) is fascinating.

The story of how that happened—how the crucifixion of Jesus turned our ethical framework upside down (or right-side up)—is fascinating, and one that has been drawing increasing attention from historians in recent years. Tom Holland's *Dominion*, for example, traces the narrative right through the centuries, and shows how many of our contemporary assumptions are fundamentally cross-shaped without people realising it, from our responses to genocide to Beatles lyrics, from sex to secularism. Holland writes:

"It is the audacity of it—the audacity of finding in a twisted and defeated corpse the glory of the creator of the universe—that

serves to explain, more surely than anything else, the sheer
strangeness of Christianity, and of the civilisation to which it
gave birth. All are heirs to the same revolution: a revolution
that has, at its molten heart, the image of a god dead on a
cross." (pages 524-525)

By dying the death of a slave and then rising again, Jesus brought
honour to the most apparently shameful people in society. He con-
founded the wisdom of the wise and the intelligence of the intelligent
while elevating humility above pride, and sacrifice above violence. Like
a pebble thrown into a pond, the cross sent ripples across the world
which gradually renewed the moral landscape, dignifying what was
despised and putting worldly power in its place. "God chose the lowly
things of this world and the despised things—and the things that are
not—to nullify the things that are, so that no one may boast before
him" (1:28-29).

We all live in the shadow of Christ crucified, whether we follow Jesus or not. Just today, and without knowing that it would be relevant
to what I am writing, I have rolled my eyes at a boastful politician,
made decisions on the basis of how they will affect poor people in
other countries, and cried while reading about the abuse suffered by
someone I have never met. All of those things are quite normal in our
world; all of them would have been quite inexplicable to most people
in Roman Corinth. And the difference between the two is the result of
this man, and this letter, and this message of Christ crucified. "Jews
demand signs and Greeks look for wisdom, but we preach Christ crucified: a stumbling-block to Jews and foolishness to Gentiles, but to
those whom God has called, both Jews and Greeks, Christ the power
of God and the wisdom of God" (v 22-24).

Questions for reflection

1. What aspect of the cross moves you the most? Why?

2. In what ways has your behaviour today been shaped by the cross, even in ways that you didn't notice at the time?

3. How might the influence of the cross in our culture, despite the fact that many people are not believers, be helpful in communicating the gospel to people?

2. SPIRITUALITY AND COMMUNITY

What you win people with is what you win them to. Youth and children's ministers know this better than anyone. Attracting a crowd is easy if you provide enough games, sweets, sports or free pizza. But if you win people with pizza then, when the pizza disappears, so do they. On the other hand, if what you are offering is Jesus Christ, then the crowd will be an awful lot smaller—but the ones who come are much more likely to become disciples. (Good youth and kids' ministry often involves elements of both, in my experience, but it is vital to be clear about how and why.)

Cross Words

Paul had no intention of giving out free pizza, but he was well aware of the dangers of attracting people to the wrong thing: "I did not come with eloquence or human wisdom as I proclaimed to you the testimony about God" (**2:1**), nor did he display an impressive sense of self-confidence (**v 3**). Crowds in the ancient world would gather much more easily around a rhetorically gifted or impassioned speaker; and in many ways they still do. But if people were gathering to eloquence or wisdom, then, when a more eloquent or educated person showed up, the crowd would disappear. (Sadly there are countless parallels in the history of Christian mission.) So "I resolved to know nothing while I was with you except Jesus Christ and him crucified" (**v 2**).

One of the puzzles of 1 Corinthians is that Paul repeatedly insists that he did not use eloquence or "wise and persuasive words" (**v 4**), yet the letter is full of some of the most powerful and eloquent rhetoric in the whole of Scripture. There is the intense sarcasm of 4:8-13, with its dramatic conclusion; the lyrical beauty of chapter 13, which may be the best-loved and most widely quoted piece of ancient literature in the world today; and sayings that we still use 20 centuries later: "the scum of the earth" (4:13), "all things to all men" (9:22), "faith that moves mountains" (13:2) and "in the twinkling of an eye" (15:52). It seems strange that in a letter packed with eloquence and wisdom Paul would so strongly deny that he ever used eloquence and wisdom.

But his point is not that using language well is bad or that he never does it himself. His point is that using language well is bad if it detracts from or substitutes for the message of Christ crucified. (There is nothing wrong with giving young people free pizza if the entire event is focused on Jesus.) Paul's priority is a demonstration of the Spirit's power (**2:4**), which in context refers to the preaching of the cross rather than the signs and wonders that some people might expect. This narrow focus is at the heart of Paul's missionary strategy, and he is crystal clear as to why: "so that your faith might not rest on human wisdom, but on God's power" (**v 5**). Again, what you win people with is what you win them to.

Unthinkable Things

The cross looks like the height of foolishness, but it is actually the height of wisdom. It is foolish in worldly terms, and always has been: bleeding, naked, impaled Jewish men are not the role models the world typically looks for. But in Christian terms the cross embodies the wisdom of God and displays the profound differences between the Creator and his creatures. In particular, the crucifixion of Christ highlights three contrasts between "this age" and the age to come, each of which are introduced in **verse 6**.

The first is familiar by now. There is a huge difference between "the wisdom of this age", which is immature and changeable, and the timeless wisdom of God, which Paul preaches and which is "a message of wisdom among the mature". Human beings are "wise" (or so we think) in very timebound ways. The popular view of what constitutes a good life changes significantly every few decades. Each generation overturns the consensus of the previous one on important subjects, not just scientifically but morally. (If you are appalled by some of the things your great-grandparents believed, don't worry: your great-grandchildren will be appalled by some of the things you believe.)

In truth, that is what immaturity looks like. Human beings, like small children, are continually drawn to new things, and we tend to be captivated by what is directly in front of us. The wisdom of God, by contrast, is timeless. It is mature, changeless and stable. It doesn't wax and wane with fashions. In previous generations it was hidden, but it was always there, "destined for our glory before time began" (**v 7**).

There is also a contrast between the "rulers of this age" and "the Lord of glory" (**v 8**). The rulers of this age—and Paul probably has in mind a combination of Caesar, Pilate, the Jewish high priests and perhaps others—were caught up in the wisdom of this age, as rulers always are. Roman rulers were committed to military power, pride, worldly glory and the brutal suppression of those who challenged them. Israel's leaders had their own wisdom, and clearly thought that sacrificing Jesus was a price worth paying for protecting the status quo (John 11:47-53). But they did not understand what God was

> At the cross, two rulers and two wisdoms collided.

doing at **Calvary**, and "if they had, they would not have crucified the Lord of glory" (1 Corinthians **2:8**).

At the cross, two rulers and two wisdoms collided. Caesar's worldly wisdom of military power and pride met Christ's divine wisdom of humility, service and sacrifice. On the Friday afternoon, Rome was triumphant. The rulers of this age looked to have won, as usual. But by

Sunday morning things looked very different. The Lord of glory was vindicated, and so was the wisdom of God.

The third contrast relates to how long each "age" will last. The wisdom and the rulers of this age are "coming to nothing" (**v 6**). This is obviously true historically, in that all rulers die, all worldly wisdom moves on, and so forth. It is also true eternally: viewed from the perspective of eternity, the insights and influencers of this age are breathtakingly short-lived. The wisdom and rule of God, on the other hand, will last for ever and be unutterably glorious: "What no eye has seen, what no ear has heard, and what no human mind has conceived—[these] things God has prepared for those who love him" (**v 9**).

This verse has been a source of comfort for many Christians, and with good reason. It reminds us that no matter how marvellous we think eternity will be, it will be beyond our powers of imagination. The reassurance for Paul, however, is not that our future cannot be imagined but that it can—but only by the Spirit's revelation: "these are the things God has revealed to us by his Spirit" (**v 10**). The Spirit, as so often in Paul's writings, is the one who provides a foretaste now of our unthinkably glorious future.

True Spirituality

If you asked people which passage in 1 Corinthians was most focused on the work of the Holy Spirit, I suspect many would point to chapters 12 and 14. Spiritual gifts like prophecy and languages are exciting, dramatic and controversial, so that is where our mind turns when we consider the Spirit's activity in this letter. But the Spirit is mentioned more in **2:10-16** than he is in the whole of chapter 12, and twice as often as he is in chapter 14. More surprisingly, his work is described here not in terms of gifting and service—though these are hugely important, and we will return to them later—but in terms of revelation, knowledge and discernment.

This is quite deliberate. Remember that Paul is writing because he is concerned with the divisions and factions in the Corinthian church (see 1:10). So, long before he talks about the gifts, which he knows are an area of disagreement and division among the Corinthians, he looks to redefine their concept of the Spirit's activity and the shape of Christian spirituality. He wants them to see that the heart of the Spirit's work is to bring the revelation of Jesus to the church—revelation which, if taken on board, will lead the Corinthians away from division and pride and towards humility and unity.

"The Spirit searches all things, even the deep things of God" (**2:10**). Theology, when done properly, is a Spirit-led and Spirit-guided exercise. We read the Scriptures, which the Spirit has inspired, in the midst of the church, whom the Spirit has filled, in search of the Christ, whom the Spirit reveals. Without the Spirit, we would have no access to the thoughts of God (**v 11**) and would end up with nothing more than the spirit of the world. With him, however, "we may understand what God has freely given us" (**v 12**). Paul is making a subtle but crucial point. The Spirit does not seek to reveal obscure practices and secret codes, let alone things which would make some Christians feel superior to others (as was happening in first-century Corinth and sadly still happens in churches today). He seeks to reveal whatever God has freely given for us to know, and he reveals it to anyone who believes.

Being truly spiritual, then, involves receiving this revelation from the Spirit and then communicating it "not in words taught us by human wisdom but in words taught by the Spirit, explaining spiritual realities with Spirit-taught words" (**v 13**). This is a good summary of Paul's goal in ministry (and his sideswipe at human wisdom suggests he is still contrasting human thinking with the cross, the ultimate "spiritual reality"). It is also a good job description for Christian pastors, missionaries and anyone else with a gospel-teaching ministry. Explaining spiritual realities with Spirit-taught words will mean you get a lot of blank faces from unspiritual people, because they have no idea what you are on about (**v 14**). But when you are talking to people of the Spirit—which here, as elsewhere in Paul's letters, means all believers rather than an elite subgroup—you will find they discern things spiritually and not just humanly (**v 15**).

In contemporary culture it is fashionable to refer to yourself as "spiritual but not religious". It means something like this: "I am spiritually open, and I know that there is more to life than the movements of atoms—but I have rejected organised religion and I'm pursuing my own path". In Paul's terms, though, such people are actually "religious but not spiritual". They are seeking meaning in the world through divine realities. They worship someone or something, even if it is just themselves. But ultimately, because they do not have the Spirit of God, they are not truly spiritual, and they have no way of understanding spiritual realities. Without the Spirit, nobody can know the mind of God, as the Old Testament quotation makes clear (**v 16**, quoting Isaiah 40:13). But because disciples of Jesus have been given the Spirit, "we have the mind of Christ".

That helps us enormously. It means that as Christians we need not feel inferior to those who claim to be spiritual—whether we encounter them in the church or in the "Mind, Body and Spirit" section of the local bookshop—because we have the Spirit of God. It means we cannot feel superior to people whose practical expression of Christianity looks different from ours (as we will see again in chapters 12 – 14). And it means we can be secure in the knowledge that God's thoughts are not out of reach. They have been made known to us in the cross of Christ, the gift of the Spirit and the revelation of the word.

Questions for reflection

1. When are you tempted to rely on human eloquence and wisdom (or pizza)? What would it look like for you to resolve to "know nothing ... except Jesus Christ and him crucified"?

2. In what ways do the beliefs and wisdom of today differ from those of previous generations? What does that tell you about earthly wisdom?

3. How is "being spiritual" usually defined? How does this passage reshape that view?

PART TWO

Babies and Plants

After opening the letter (1:1-9) and introducing the problem he is going to be addressing (1:10-17), Paul has spent a long time contrasting the wisdom of God with the wisdom of the world, primarily through the cross of Christ (1:18-2:5) and the ministry of the Spirit (2:6-18). He wants behavioural change, but he wants it to be built on theological foundations. With that platform established, he now turns in **3:1-9** to address the divisions and factions in the church more directly, using two metaphors for the Corinthian believers. One of them is a lot less flattering than the other.

In the first, he calls them babies (**v 1**); the word he uses is *nepioi*, from which we get the English word "nappy" (a diaper, if you are in the US). Like squabbling toddlers, they are characterised by jealousy and quarrelling (**v 3**). Some claim to follow Paul, while others claim to follow Apollos (**v 4**). This behaviour is clearly immature and explains why Paul had to start the letter by reminding them of the basics of the cross, as opposed to the meaty challenges he will give them later: "I gave you milk, not solid food, for you were not yet ready for it" (**v 2**). But it is also "worldly"—fleshly or **carnal** (**v 3**). For all their pride in being "spiritual", the Corinthians are actually as fleshly as anyone.

Some interpreters have taken this to mean that there are three different groups when it comes to the Spirit: genuinely spiritual Christians (like Paul), carnal or worldly Christians (like the Corinthians), and unbelievers. This is not what Paul is saying at all, and it would completely undermine the point he was making in 2:10-16. Rather, Paul is using the Corinthians' language—"spiritual" and "fleshly", "mature" and "immature"—to challenge them about their divisiveness. *You like to think you are spiritual and mature,* he is saying, *and that you understand the deep, meaty things of God rather than depending on milky baby food. But when you squabble and divide like this, which are you really?*

In **3:5-9**, Paul changes the metaphor from a baby to a plant and shifts the focus from the Corinthians to himself and Apollos. It is not just that they need a lower view of themselves; they also need a lower view of human leaders, who are merely "servants, through whom you came to believe" (**v 5**). Paul planted a seed by preaching the gospel in Corinth in the first place. Apollos watered it by following up after Paul left town. But it is God who gives the spiritual growth (**v 6**) and therefore God who should get all the credit. Putting too much stock by human leaders shows a misunderstanding of where the growth really comes from.

It is a powerful picture, and one with plenty of application to the contemporary Western church. Like the Corinthians, we risk elevating human leaders and giving too much credit to people who are merely farm labourers and servants. Like the Corinthians, we are prone to see pastors and their ministries as in competition with one another, where Paul sees them all as "fellow workers"—both with each other and with God himself—who all have "one purpose" (**v 8-9**). Like the Corinthians, we can slip into thinking that the reward for Christian ministry comes from among us in the present—whether in the form of recognition or payment—rather than from God in the future, when "each [will] be rewarded according to their own labour" (**v 8**). And like the Corinthians, we can see church growth as the result of a preference for a particular sort of leader or experience rather than as a divine miracle in which a field is scattered with gospel seed and only produces life through the powerful work of God. The humbling yet encouraging truth is that "neither the one who plants nor the one who waters is anything, but only God, who makes things grow" (**v 7**).

Build Carefully

So far, the individuals responsible for the factions within the Corinthian church have not been challenged directly. The sense we have from the first two chapters is that the entire church is at fault; everyone is causing division by aligning themselves with human leaders, and everyone is boasting about them in a way that conflicts with both the gospel of Christ crucified and the work of the Spirit. In **verses 10-15** that starts to change. We are still not given any names, but we begin to realise that Paul has some specific individuals in mind. Certain leaders within the community are particularly responsible for the chaos, and Paul intends to warn them about what they are doing.

He raises the issue with yet another metaphor. The church is a house, he says, made of all sorts of building materials. The expert builder who laid the groundwork is Paul himself, when he first preached the gospel to the Corinthians (**v 10**). Ever since, everyone who has preached or led within the church has been building on that foundation, which, of course, is Jesus Christ (**v 11**). In theory, building the church is a great opportunity for teamwork. Paul got things started by preaching Christ and then moved on to Ephesus, at which point other builders in Corinth—pastors, teachers, leaders in the congregation—took over. In practice, though, it is easy for these new builders to make a mess of things, seeking their own agenda rather than the good of the church and bringing division rather than unity. So "each one should build with care" (**v 10**).

> In theory, building the church is a great opportunity for teamwork. In practice, it is easy to make a mess of things.

If they do, they have nothing to worry about. When the fiery day of judgment comes, their work in the gospel will be shown for what it is (**v 12-13**). If they have built with gold, silver and costly stones— if they have preached Christ, loved one another, pursued unity and obeyed the Spirit—then the fire will simply reveal quite how well they have "built" the church (**v 14**). Careful building, of the kind that Paul and Apollos have displayed, will result in a church that survives and a reward for the builders.

But there is another possibility. If they have built poorly, with wood, hay or straw—if they have preached worldly wisdom rather than the cross and led with pride, fostered division and been shaped by the spirit of the world—then when the fiery judgment comes, their ministry will be exposed as a sham and go up in flames (**v 15**). Tragically it is not hard to think of pastors like that today: people whose pride and worldliness have damaged entire churches. In situations like this, Paul says, the builder will still be saved—but only just, like a person being rescued from a burning house.

This verse is the main text that Roman Catholics appeal to in support of the **doctrine** of **purgatory**. But that is not what Paul is not talking about here. The fire in the metaphor does not purge a person; it tests the quality of their work (and specifically their work in building the church), either revealing it to be good or exposing it as poor. It is not a passage about post-mortem purification at all.

In some ways a closer equivalent is the story of the Three Little Pigs. Some of us build with straw, some with wood, and some with bricks. When the time of judgment comes—"I'll huff and I'll puff and I'll blow your house down"—the quality of the building is revealed. If it has been built with bricks, it survives. If it is built with straw it collapses, and even though (in most tellings of the tale) the little pig survives, huge damage is done. Paul is saying to the key people in the Corinthian church, "Each one should build with care" (**v 10**).

Do Not Destroy

Gradually, in chapter 3, Paul has been turning up the heat. Initially he pictured the church as a field, and Christian leaders as farm workers who will be "rewarded according to their labour" (**v 5-9**). Then he portrayed it as a house, and Christian leaders as builders who might be rewarded but who might also "suffer loss" if they built carelessly, despite ultimately being saved (**v 10-15**). In both cases, the final salvation of the leader was not under threat.

In **verses 16-23**, that changes. The church is now described as the dwelling place of God himself: "Don't you know that you yourselves are God's temple, and that God's Spirit lives among you?" (**v 16**). Temples are not ordinary buildings where you can do what you like; they represent sacred space, and in the Old Testament, people who approached God's presence inappropriately faced immediate punishment or even death (for instance, Leviticus 10:1-2; 2 Samuel 6:5-9; 2 Chronicles 26:16-21). That should affect the way we think about our local churches, and as this letter continues Paul gives us various examples: our response to sexual sin (1 Corinthians 5:1-5), our sharing of the Lord's Supper (11:17-34), our use of spiritual gifts (12:1-31), and so on. Here, the divisive leaders are warned not just as careless builders of a house but as active destroyers of a temple. And the consequences of doing this—of destroying God's church—are drastic: "If anyone destroys God's temple, God will destroy that person; for God's temple is sacred" (**3:17**). Shoddy workmanship in building up the people of God—the church—causes damage to everyone, but it doesn't disqualify a person from salvation. Destroying the church, on the other hand, most definitely does. Paul doesn't tell us whether the difference between the two is the extent of the damage, the wilfulness of it, or something else, but his language here should make us want to err on the side of caution.

Warning and Assurance

This is the first of several passages in the letter that warn believers away from eternal destruction. We will encounter several others in due course, most strikingly in chapter 10. At the same time, Paul has already guaranteed the Corinthians that God will keep them strong to the end and present them blameless on the day of Christ (1:7-9), and he will later reassure them that their resurrection from the dead is certain through the resurrection of Jesus (15:20-28). So we have a tension here. Is Paul warning believers away from eternal destruction (chapters 3, 6 and 10), or is he assuring them that they will inherit eternal glory (chapters 1 and 15)?

The answer is both. Because of the faithfulness of God, the resurrection of Christ and the activity of the Spirit, Paul is certain that the Corinthians will be preserved for future salvation. But he is equally certain that some behaviour—destroying the church, unrepentant sexual or financial sin, worshipping idols and so on—will lead to eternal judgment. There is a tension here, and Paul knows it. The best way of making sense of it, I think, is to see Paul's warnings as the God-given way in which the Corinthians will be preserved in faith. These passages are like a sign that says, "Warning: Touching This Cable Will Kill You". Paul is clear that destroying the church is a life-or-death matter. He is also confident that, by the grace of God, the Corinthians will listen, repent, and avoid the destruction he is talking about.

But that requires an immediate response. These Christians must stop kidding themselves that they are wise and get back in line with the "foolishness" of God revealed in the cross (**3:18-20**). And they must stop boasting in human leaders, whether Paul, Apollos, Cephas, or anyone else (**v 21-22**). These two are obviously connected. Boasting in leaders is something you only do if you have a worldly concept of wisdom; if your view of wisdom is godly, spiritual and cross-shaped, as Paul laid it out in chapters 1 and 2, it will lead you towards humble unity rather than haughty infighting.

Boastfulness, factionalism and pride are destructive to everybody. They destroy the individuals who participate in them, and, left unchecked, they destroy the church as a whole. The good news, Paul says, is that they are also completely unnecessary. There is no need to insist that Paul is "yours" or Apollos is "mine" (**3:21**). If you are in Christ, then everything belongs to you already: human leaders, life and death, the present and the future, and the entire world (**v 22**). When we think our inheritance is small and insignificant, we squabble like toddlers over every last bit of it. When we lift up our eyes and see how much is ours in Christ, our tribal allegiances fade into the background, as when **Abraham** gave **Lot** the best bit of land because he knew that God would give him everything else (Genesis 13). That is why Paul ends a fairly heavy chapter with such an uplifting conclusion: "All [things] are yours, and you are of Christ, and Christ is of God" (1 Corinthians **3:22-23**).

Questions for reflection

1. In what ways do people in the church put human leaders on a pedestal? How are you most likely to do that?

2. What do you think it means for Christian leaders to "build with care"? Why is this so important?

3. As you reflect on this passage, what will you pray for your church?

3. DISCIPLINE IN THEORY AND IN PRACTICE

One of the intriguing challenges of being a pastor in a post-Christian country like mine is how to explain your job to people outside the church. Some people already know what a pastor is. Plenty of others have enough exposure to the church to have some context for what you do, even if they imagine something very different from what the job actually involves in practice. But sometimes you find yourself talking to people who have absolutely no idea. I remember saying I was a pastor to a group of fellow postgraduate students, and finding there was not a single person there who had even heard the word.

Working out what to say next when you are in that situation is quite a helpful exercise. It shows what you really think Christian ministry is. I have friends who describe it as "helping people explore spirituality". The writer Eugene Peterson tells of a colleague who said simply, "I run a church". (Peterson was horrified. He said many years later, "I can still distinctly remember the unpleasant impression it made".) In American-influenced culture, many pastors use terms like "leader", "director" or even "executive", drawing on terminology from the business world to explain their role. This language has the advantage of being clear to people who are not believers, but it runs the risk of letting the corporate world reshape Christian ministry in its own image. (If you go to enough church-leadership conferences, you'll find this has happened fairly dramatically in some circles.)

Paul's description of his role is revealing. "This, then, is how you ought to regard us: as servants of Christ and as those entrusted with the mysteries God has revealed" (**4:1**). He wants to be viewed as a servant and a steward: a man to whom the revelation of God has been entrusted, and who has a responsibility to proclaim it wherever he goes. In other words, he is a trustee. God has given him an enormously valuable resource—the gospel of Jesus Christ—and it is Paul's job to "prove faithful" (**v 2**), by stewarding that resource diligently and preaching it faithfully. It is not actually his. It belongs to God, and that means it has to be stewarded in God's interests, not Paul's (let alone those of the Corinthians).

It also means that his accountability is to God, rather than the Corinthians (**v 3-4**). As we have seen, people in the congregation have been aligning themselves with specific human leaders, including Paul, and presumably expecting certain things in return for their allegiance. (Later in the Corinthian letters we discover that some of them are using money to express that allegiance in practical ways. This is one of the reasons why Paul refuses to accept it—see 2 Corinthians 11:1-15.) His response is simple: *In the end my ministry—my trusteeship, if you like, of the mysteries of God in Christ—will be judged by God, not by you lot. I know that some of you don't approve of the way I approach these matters, but ultimately I don't work for you. I work for God. I am waiting for his judgment.* The fact that some leaders have abused this text, taking it as a licence to ignore the wise counsel and correction of their fellow pastors and church members, should make us very wary of playing this card ourselves—but we should not miss the truth of what Paul is saying either. On that day everything hidden will come to light, the motives of every heart will be made plain and everyone will receive praise from God accordingly (1 Corinthians **4:5**).

In operating this way, part of Paul's motivation is to show the church what it means "not [to] go beyond what is written" (**v 6**). This might be the single most confusing verse in the letter, because the Greek is a bit of a grammatical tangle, and it is hard to be certain what he is referring to. But I think Paul is saying that his approach to ministry is designed to show the importance of living according to Scripture, and of refusing to "go beyond" it in the face of worldly pressure. And I think the Scriptures he has in mind are the ones he has referred to already about the foolishness of human wisdom (1:19; 3:19-20), the wonder and incomprehensibility of divine wisdom (2:9, 16) and the importance of only boasting in the Lord (1:31). By ministering as he does, Paul wants to make plain the power of living by the word of God—and in particular of living by its teaching on humility and wisdom, so that "you will not be puffed up in being a follower of one of us over against the other" (**4:6**).

As he concludes this section, he asks one of the most beautiful questions in the entire Bible: "What do you have that you did not receive?" (**v 7**). This is Pauline theology in a sentence. All is grace. Everything the Corinthians have—and everything Paul has, and everything we have—is a gift of God. The cross, the Spirit, the wisdom of God made known in Christ, any knowledge or insight that they have... they are all gifts. None of us have earned them, and none of us deserve them. Grace, more than any other Christian teaching, pulls the rug out from under our self-reliance, our boasting and our pride. If everything we have has been given to us by God, then how on earth can we boast as if it is somehow ours by right?

Cross-shaped Apostles

Christians are often surprised to find sarcasm and irony in the Bible. It may feel that the word of God should contain only careful, earnest, logical arguments or worthy principles to live by, but not ironic jokes or sarcastic rants. Yet if you read the teachings of Jesus for more than a few minutes, you'll quickly see that there is humour and irony everywhere. But the two most sarcastic passages in Scripture are in the Corinthian letters: the famous "fool's speech" (2 Corinthians 11:16 – 12:10) and this passage here in 1 Corinthians **4:8-13**.

"Already you have all you want! Already you have become rich! You have begun to reign ... How I wish that you really had begun to reign so that we also might reign with you!" (**v 8**). This is ridicule, plain and simple. We mustn't try and rescue Paul from his words here; he is making fun of the Corinthians. Like a political satirist, he is bursting the bubble of their pretensions to worldly wisdom, leadership, honour and status.

> We mustn't try to rescue Paul from his words; he is making fun of the Corinthians.

We saw what he really thinks of their social standing in chapter 1. When God saved them, the Corinthians weren't especially smart, rich, powerful or high-powered (1:26-31). Here, however, he describes them as rich rulers who have everything they could possibly want (**4:8**): they are wise, strong and honoured (**v 10**). Some interpreters take this as evidence that the Corinthians held to "over-realised eschatology": the idea that they were already living in the future kingdom of Christ, ruling and reigning, with all they could ever need (see for example Fee, *The First Epistle to the Corinthians*, pages 16-17). (This interpretation also explains their view of sex and marriage, their obsession with tongue-speaking, and their denial of the future resurrection.) Others, with whom I agree, think these problems are more connected by worldliness than by confused eschatology (see for example Barclay, *Thessalonica and Corinth*, in JSNT 47, pages 49-74). Either way, in this passage Paul does not respond by correcting their eschatology. He responds by skewering their self-importance.

Primarily, he does this by contrasting them with "us apostles" (**v 9**). This "us" here refers to "myself and Apollos" (**v 6**), whom Paul mentions in order to prevent the various factions in the church from playing the apostles off against each other. (If you're a parent, you will have done this yourself. Children always go to Mum if Dad says no, and vice versa, so you learn to say things like "Your father and I have decided …") *You Corinthians are all kings, but we apostles are condemned men on our way to be killed in the arena,* Paul says. *You* *have everything you want, but we are publicly humiliated and shamed in front of angels and humans alike (**v 9**). We are foolish, weak and dishonoured (**v 10**). We have nothing to eat, nothing to wear, no way of defending ourselves and nowhere to live (**v 11**). Our only response to slander and persecution is to endure it and bless our oppressors (**v 12**). We are the scum of the earth, the muck that you scrape off the bottom of your shoe (**v 13**).*

Paul is not calling for pity here. He is not playing the victim card. (In the ancient world, which had not yet been transformed by Christian morality, there was no victim card to play in the first place.) What he is doing, without ever mentioning the word "cross", is reminding them that at the heart of the gospel is the shamed, brutalised and humiliated Son of Man, who had nowhere to lay his head—and that Christians take their cue from him rather than from those whom the world elevates and admires. The Corinthians, in seeking and promoting the wisdom, honour, wealth and status of the world, have Christianity completely upside down.

They were not the only ones. You do not have to look far in the contemporary church to see success defined in exactly the same ways as it is in the world: numbers, downloads, budgets, bums on seats, book sales, academic qualifications, buildings, celebrity attendance, worldly influence. None of these things are necessarily wrong. But those of us who have them—which to some extent includes me—need to examine our hearts frequently in light of 1 Corinthians 4, and in light of the cross to which it points, to see whether we have flipped the gospel on its head without realising it. I often think of the **apocryphal** story in which the 12th-century founder of the Dominican order of monks, St Dominic, visits the Pope, who is surrounded by all the wealth and splendour of early medieval Rome. The Pope, so the story goes, refers to Acts 3:1-10 and boasts that Peter can no longer say, "Silver and gold I do not have". "No indeed," replies St Dominic, "but then again, neither can he say, 'Rise up and walk'".

Discipleship and Discipline

The previous paragraph saw Paul on fairly bombastic form, and he knows it. Pastoral care needs to be robust sometimes; admonishing people does not always sound as polite or affirming as our culture might like. But next he changes his tone quite abruptly and reassures the church that his intention is not to shame them but to warn them (1 Corinthians **4:14**). His language moves from sarcasm to intimacy. The Corinthians are his "dear children". Even if they had ten thousand guardians in Christ, Paul would remain their father because he was the one who first preached the gospel to them (**v 15**). So he urges them to imitate him—again, by pursuing unity, humility and the foolishness of the cross rather than the divisive, boastful arrogance of worldly Corinth—just as children imitate their parents (**v 16**). Like father, like son.

Having said that, it is tricky to imitate someone who is not physically present. This is a problem Paul faced throughout his ministry: after preaching the gospel and establishing a local church, he would either be forced to skip town and do the same thing somewhere else or he would get thrown into jail for disturbing public order. So after the initial period of ministry he was not accessible to his churches, and that made it much harder for them to imitate him. Discipleship is difficult from a distance. (This is one reason why, despite Paul's itinerant example, the normal pattern of New Testament church life is to have local pastors who stay in one place for many years.)

To address this, Paul is sending them Timothy, "my son whom I love, who is faithful in the Lord" (**v 17**). Timothy's role is to be a bridge between Paul and the Corinthians, and a reminder of Paul's way of life, "which agrees with what I teach everywhere in every church". That is a fairly brief introduction—Timothy will not be mentioned again until the very end of the letter—but it makes two vital points about the way disciples are made and formed. One is that disciples are ultimately made by people. They are not primarily made by ideas, or teachings, or letters (even if those are from the apostle Paul himself);

they are made by real, tangible human people who embody the gospel as well as preaching it. The other is that discipleship is a combination of doctrine ("what I teach everywhere") and practice ("my way of life"). Good teaching is essential, but transformation happens when people not only teach but actually live out the Christian faith in front of us, showing us how the cross shapes our work, our relationships and our finances, and in this case our unity and humility in Christ.

The challenges in this particular church remain severe. Paul knows that even Timothy will struggle to correct them all, given the arrogance being shown by some (**v 18**). So he plans to follow up with a visit himself, God willing, "and then I will find out not only how these arrogant people are talking, but what power they have" (**v 19**).

That could sound like trash talk, like a boxer or a wrestler before a big fight. ("He may say that in the media, but let's see what happens when we get in the ring together!") It is actually the opposite. We later discover that the Corinthians do not think much of Paul's speech when he comes in person (2 Corinthians 10:10), and Paul insists that the one thing he does not want is a war of words, because the kingdom is not about words but power (1 Corinthians **4:20**). So in planning to visit them, he isn't hoping for a showdown at all. He is hoping to visit "in love and with a gentle spirit" (**v 21**). But like any good father, he is prepared to use discipline if he has to. Given how far the Corinthians' boasting has reached, this is a very real possibility.

It makes us wonder: what on earth are the Corinthians boasting about, that he has to speak this forcefully? Surely it cannot be that bad, can it? As we reach chapter 5, we are about to find out.

Questions for reflection

1. "It is the Lord who judges me" (v 4). How does this change the way you view your own efforts to serve God and his church? Do you find it liberating or challenging—or both?

2. Are there ways in which you are impressive in the world's eyes? Or do you feel particularly unimpressive? Either way, how will you make sure you boast in Christ alone?

3. Who are you influenced by, and whom do you influence? Do you need to make any changes either to the examples you follow or the example you provide?

PART TWO

Incest and Pride

Imagine a man in your church is in an incestuous sexual relationship with his stepmother (**5:1**). He is a fairly well-known person in the congregation and has always professed to be a believer. Everybody in the church knows about it; the couple have moved in together. Word is now getting out more widely: members of your church have mentioned it to friends of theirs in other churches, sometimes in other countries. Even people in your city who are not Christians are raising their eyebrows at the news. How do you respond?

The Corinthians' response is to be proud of it (**v 2**). We are not told why, but it is probably caused by a combination of three factors: a distorted view of Christian freedom (6:12; 10:23-24), a woefully deficient vision of human sexuality (much of chapters 6 and 7), and the elevated social status of the man in question. Powerful people get a free pass in many societies. In an **honour-shame culture**, and in a city where sexual promiscuity was so widespread that the comic playwright Aristophanes had coined the verb *korinthiazo*—to "Corinthianise", or fornicate—powerful patrons must have been nearly untouchable. The modern parallels are uncomfortable.

Paul's response is to be doubly outraged. He is appalled by the sin itself, explaining that this kind of thing isn't tolerated even among pagans (**5:1**). Far more seriously, he is outraged by the response of the church and spends most of his time addressing the pride rather than the incest, and the church as a community rather than the incestuous couple. We may find that surprising. We might be more worried by the individual than the whole—by the egregious sin rather than the widespread acceptance (or even celebration) of it. But Paul's chief concern is for the integrity of the church. His response, which he will elaborate in the rest of the chapter, is summarised in **verse 2**: "Shouldn't you rather have gone into mourning and have put out of your fellowship the man who has been doing this?" So begins one of the most important passages in the New Testament on church discipline.

It is not that Paul is trivialising the immorality. Though physically absent, Paul is with them in spirit and is clear that he has "already passed judgment in the name of the Lord Jesus on the one who has been doing this" (**v 3**; the fact that he refers to the "one" who did this implies that although the man is part of the church, the stepmother is not). But Paul wants their verdict on the incest to match his own. He wants the church to express publicly what he is writing personally (**v 4**): that the sin is grievous, that they mourn for it and will have nothing to do with it, and that consequently they will remove the offending man from the church.

The phrase he uses is a vivid and striking one: "Hand this man over to Satan" (**v 5**). It sounds terrifying, and in many ways it is. But Paul is not thinking of dark magic here, in which the church gets together and casts a spell on the man, let alone any of the horror-movie rituals and weirdnesses that might follow. Rather, like the Old Testament, he is thinking in terms of sacred space, in which sin is removed from the place where God has chosen to live (Eden, the tabernacle, the temple, the church) and cast out into the place where Satan still holds sway (exile, the wilderness, the land outside the camp, the world). As such, "hand this man over to Satan" is simply another way of saying *Put this man out of your fellowship* (**v 2**) or "expel the wicked person from among you" (**v 13**).

The goal of this process is twofold. The first part is obvious from the NIV's translation: "... for the destruction of the flesh, so that his spirit may be saved on the day of the Lord" (**v 5**). Excluding someone from fellowship may seem harsh, but it is aimed at bringing the person to their senses, so that their flesh—their sinful nature, their illicit desires, their rebellion and immorality—may be destroyed, and they may reach a point of repentance and so find salvation. This is not automatic. It is not as if the act of kicking people out of the church will save them all by itself. But that outcome is what Paul hopes for in the case of this man. It is also what he hopes for in 1 Timothy 1:20, the only other place where he talks about a similar action—that of handing people over to Satan "so that they may learn not to **blaspheme**".

Paul's other purpose in this process is hinted at by the fact that he does not talk about destroying "his" flesh or saving "his" spirit, but about destroying "the" flesh and saving "the" spirit (or even "the Spirit", although I doubt that Paul would talk about the Holy Spirit being "saved"). For that reason, some interpreters think that Paul is talking about the church here (see Thiselton, *The First Epistle to the Corinthians*, pages 396-400; Yinger, *Paul, Judaism and Judgment According to Deeds*, pages 240-244). The expulsion of this man is not only aimed at destroying what is fleshly in him but also at destroying what is fleshly within the Corinthian church and saving that which is spiritual among them. This also fits with Paul's concern throughout the chapter. As we will see in the next section, this man's sin has the potential to destroy not just him but the entire congregation.

> One thing that makes Paul such a compelling thinker and wise pastor is that he always sees the big picture.

Passover People

One of the things that makes Paul such a compelling thinker, and such a wise pastor, is that he always sees the big picture. When challenging sin, it is surprisingly easy to zoom in on the specifics of the behaviour and surprisingly difficult to zoom out and see the whole spiritual, historical and cosmological canvas on which it is painted. (This ability to zoom out is critical in our generation, when so many people are, like the Corinthians, challenging biblical teaching on sex and sexuality.) I don't know how you would challenge a church that had accepted incest among its members, or which passages of Scripture you would appeal to. My guess is that I would have zoomed in on a specific in-struction, like "Do not have sexual relations with your father's wife; that would dishonour your father" (Leviticus 18:8), and left it at that.

Paul zooms out. He starts not with Leviticus but with Exodus. He be-gins with gospel rather than with law. He heads for the defining event of the Old Testament Scriptures—the escape from Egypt by means of the **Passover**—and uses it to show why the church must not be compromised and defiled by unrepented immorality in its midst. I say "unrepented" because it is important to remember that the problem here is not just the sin but the fact that everyone has responded to it with pride rather than grief. If this man, after having sex with his stepmother, was to repent of it and change his ways, Paul would be commending him rather than expelling him, and urging the church to welcome him back. This is exactly what happens in a different situa-tion in 2 Corinthians 2:5-11.

On the night that they escaped from Egypt, Paul explains, Israel ate unleavened bread. It was free from the fungus (yeast) which otherwise spreads throughout the dough and affects the whole loaf (1 Corin-thians **5:6**). At the very beginning of their journey to freedom, God gave Israel a meal to teach them that they were to be distinct from the world around them, and free from things that might otherwise infect God's holy people and spread throughout the whole nation. *The same is true of you and the church,* says Paul.

Since most of us don't think of yeast as a pollutant and quite enjoy bread with yeast in it, we might get a better sense of Paul's picture if we paraphrased it as "a little mould spreads throughout the whole cheese". Tolerating the mould, or the yeast, jeopardises the whole batch. The only way to save the cheese is to get rid of the mould. *And that,* Paul is saying to the Corinthians, *is what you must do with this man. You are a Passover people. You are called to be pure, undefiled, unleavened, and holy, and this is in fact what you already are.* Christ himself has been sacrificed for them as a Passover lamb, pure and without blemish (**v 7**). So when they celebrate the "festival"—which I take to be the **Lord's**

Supper here—they must not be "leavened" with malice or evil, but be pure and "unleavened" with sincerity and truth (**v 8**). Otherwise the sin of this man, and their acceptance of it, will spread throughout the whole church like yeast through a loaf or like mould through a cheese, and they will be destroyed from the inside out.

Who Are You to Judge?

Here we are, five chapters into Paul's "first" letter to the Corinthians, and in **verse 9** we suddenly discover that it is actually his second. We no longer have the previous letter he refers to. In fact, the only thing we know about it comes right here: Paul had told them "not to associate with sexually immoral people". Apparently the church had misunderstood this—or maybe pretended they had—to mean that Paul was telling them to avoid all contact with sexually immoral people. As Paul admits, that would be impossible. Cities are chock-full of people whose sexual, financial and religious lives are utterly incompatible with following Jesus, and avoiding them would mean leaving the world altogether (**v 10**).

What he meant was that they should "not associate with anyone who bears the name of brother or sister but is sexually immoral or greedy, an idolater or slanderer, a drunkard or a swindler" (**v 11**, ESV). Interacting with sexually immoral people in the world is inevitable. If people don't follow Jesus, then it's no surprise that they don't live by his rules, and it isn't our business to judge them (**v 12**). But in the church it is to be different. We bear the name of brother or sister. And if we call ourselves brothers and sisters, then we should be held to account on that basis. (The word Paul uses for "bears the name of" brother or sister, *onomazomenos*, has the sense of "so-called" brother or sister, which may mean that he thinks the incestuous man is not actually a believer. Even so, the man is purporting to be one, so he needs to be removed from the church.)

So far in this chapter Paul has described the removal of this man in a number of different ways. He has referred to putting him out of the fellowship, handing him over to Satan, getting rid of the old yeast and not associating with immoral so-called believers. In the final few sentences of this chapter, he adds three more. He talks about the need to "judge those inside" the church (**v 12**) as opposed to those outside it, which is an important challenge to all of us (especially since most of us instinctively do the opposite, condemning the world for its ungodly ways while giving our own sin a free pass). He urges them to "expel the wicked person from among you" (**v 13**), which is a direct quotation from Deuteronomy 13:5 and elsewhere, and shows how closely he associates the church with ancient Israel. And in the most jarring example, at least for many people today, he tells them, "Do not even eat with such people" (1 Corinthians **5:11**).

It is a challenging text for us, especially when we consider that Paul is not just talking about sins that are generally rejected in our culture (like incest) but also sins that are generally accepted in our culture (like sexual immorality and drunkenness)—not to mention sins that are often accepted in the church itself (like greed and slander). "Do not even eat with such people." Does he mean that we need to shun people if they are guilty of unrepented sin? Avoid their houses? Blank them in the street?

Probably not. If we consider the rest of the chapter, and the references to the gathered assembly (**v 4**), the unleavened bread of the Passover (**v 7**) and the feast we celebrate (**v 8**), it is more likely that Paul is talking about excommunication here: the act of excluding people from taking Communion with us. As we will see later on in chapters 10 and 11, sharing the Lord's Supper carries deep meaning for all who participate, and if done carelessly causes all sorts of damage to the church. By commanding the Corinthians not to eat with this man, Paul is seeking to protect them—and perhaps even him—from abusing the **Eucharist** and allowing sin to defile the **Lord's Table**. Practically that means that all of us, not just the pastors or paid staff, have a responsibility to challenge sin in one another when we see it, along the lines that Jesus lays out in Matthew 18:15-20.

Questions for reflection

1. Why is it easier to tolerate unrepented sin than to challenge it?

2. Paul zooms out to include the context of the Passover (v 6-8). Why is zooming out like this a helpful way of challenging someone's sin?

3. What could you do to take sin more seriously—both in your own life and in your church?

4. SEX AND THE CITY

The catalogue of problems at Corinth is only just beginning. Having dealt at length with pride and division (chapters 1 – 4) and the Corinthians' boastful response to incest (chapter 5), Paul moves on to deal with two more issues in this chapter: suing one another and visiting prostitutes. It seems that he is working through the things he has heard about, probably through an oral report from Chloe's household (1:11), before turning to address the things the Corinthians have asked about in their letter (7:1 onwards).

There is an interesting connection between the lawsuits we read about here and the incestuous man in the previous chapter, and it is one that has a lot to teach us in our age of tolerance. In both cases, the Corinthians have made a mess of things by abdicating their responsibility to judge. They have failed to judge sin within the church by not expelling the so-called brother (5:11-13). And they have failed to take responsibility for judging disputes within the church, choosing instead to involve the law courts (**6:1-8**). People often quote Jesus' command "Do not judge" (Matthew 7:1) as if it means that we are supposed to avoid moral discernment altogether. That is not Jesus' point at all—he is talking about the superiority and pride that look down on other people's sins as worse than ours—and Paul makes it clear here that if we refuse to make judgments within the church, we can do great harm to one another. "If any of you has a dispute with another, do you dare to take it before the ungodly for judgment instead of before the Lord's people?" (1 Corinthians **6:1**).

There are a number of reasons why litigation within the church is so destructive. The first is obvious to anyone who has been in a church when this has happened: the disunity and pain caused when one person takes another to court, and the other church members get drawn into taking sides, is incalculable. It can split a church. If it doesn't, it can lead to suspicion and hostility for years, poisoning the congregation when they pray, sing, take Communion and so on. Paul has addressed the need for unity at some length already, so he does not go into it here.

The second reason is that such litigation implies that the judgments of unbelievers are more valuable than the judgments of the church, when in reality the reverse is true. The people of God are going to judge the world (**v 2**). They are going to judge angels (**v 3**): J.B. Lightfoot's comment is helpful here: "Just as the faithful shall reign with Christ as kings (2 Timothy 2:12; Revelation 22:5), so they shall sit with him as judges of the world" (*Notes on the Epistles of St. Paul*, page 210). They have the knowledge of God, the mind of Christ and the presence of the Spirit. Surely a matter like this—and we are not told what it is, but it probably involves a wealthier member throwing their legal weight around at the expense of a poorer one—is within their capability? Yet here they are, outsourcing judgment to people "whose way of life is scorned in the church" (1 Corinthians **6:4**). Paul cannot believe it.

The third reason is the shame that comes from having unbelievers seeing all the church's dirty laundry. *Given how wise you all are,* Paul says with more than a hint of sarcasm, *you would think that someone might be wise enough to sort this all out (**v 5**). Instead, you are airing all your squabbles "in front of unbelievers" (**v 6**) and showing them just how divided and selfish you are.*

And the fourth reason is that suing each other shows that you care more about being vindicated in court, with the money and social reward which that brings, than you do about your brothers and sisters (**v 7**). *Surely,* Paul is saying, *if you were looking at this through the lens*

of the cross, you would rather be cheated than divided? Isn't it bet-
ter to be defrauded in worldly terms than defeated in spiritual terms?
You are so concerned not to lose out to a wrongdoer that you have
become wrongdoers yourselves (**v 8**).

Given the scandals of the last few years in virtually every part of the
church, it is worth highlighting one thing that this passage definitely
does not mean. It does not mean that we should deal with criminal
activity in-house, without informing the police of illegal behaviour.
(The difference between civil and criminal law, and the difference between modern courts and the status- and patronage-based system in
the ancient world, are both important here.) Paul would be horrified if
we were to use this passage as a pretext for cover-ups, institutional silence or the protection of abusive leaders when serious allegations are
made. He is saying that if I have a dispute with my Christian plumber,
I should handle it within the church, perhaps using mediation or an
equivalent process, rather than suing him or her in the courts; he is
not saying that a claim of sexual abuse should be hidden from the
police and resolved by the **elders** instead. As we have seen with tragic
frequency, that sort of response leads to exactly the outcomes—division, pain and shame upon the church's reputation—that Paul has
written this section to avoid.

Transformed Lives

The lawsuit scandal brings Paul to his third major warning in the letter, after the warnings against careless or destructive building in the
church (3:10-17) and tolerating incest (5:1-13). If we are reading at-
tentively, there are several clues that it is coming. Whenever Paul says
"do you not know" (**6:9**) in this letter, there is a correction coming
(5:6; **6:2, 3, 15, 16, 19**; 9:24). It functions like an astonished "surely
you know that?" Similar things are true of "do not be deceived" (**6:9**),
which we saw the last time Paul warned against eternal destruction
(3:18). The nature of sin is that it deceives us into thinking it is not

that serious. Paul pleads with the Corinthians not to allow deception to dilute the severity of what they are doing.

Then there is his use of the word "wrongdoers." This is a great translation of *adikoi* (usually translated as "unrighteous") because it helps us see the connection between suffering wrong (**6:7**), doing wrong (**v 8**), and being "wrongdoers" (**v 9**). Paul wants us to join the dots. There are times when you have to choose between suffering wrong and doing wrong—when you are tempted to sue your brother or sister, for instance—and in those circumstances you should avoid doing wrong at all costs, because wrongdoers will not inherit the kingdom. In some traditions, this warning is interpreted as if it doesn't apply to Christians, but the verbal connection here makes clear that it does.

Although the lawsuits serve as the trigger for Paul to write this, it is not the only instance of wrongdoing that he has in mind. He mentions ten different categories of unrighteousness which disqualify a person from the kingdom (**v 9-10**). The sexually immoral: those who have any form of sexual intercourse outside of marriage between a husband and a wife. Idolaters: worshippers of any gods besides the Lord. (Paul will return to both of these in this letter.) Adulterers: married people who have sex with someone other than their spouse. Men who have sex with men: again the NIV does a great job here by making it clear that the problem is having gay sex rather than being attracted to people of the same sex. (The two Greek words here, *arsenokoitai* and *malakoi*, refer to those who penetrate males and men who are soft or effeminate.) Thieves. The greedy: people whose hearts always want more, and who use their powers to get it. (Paul may still have the Corinthian lawsuits in mind here.) Drunkards. Slanderers: those who lie about others. Swindlers: those who cheat others. *People who live like this*, Paul says, *will not inherit the kingdom of God.*

Three things are worth noting about this catalogue of wrongdoing. The first is that it ought not to be that controversial. There are no curveballs here. It is one of several lists like this in Paul's writings—he tends to tailor them according to the issues in the church he is writing to. This list covers sins that are prohibited numerous times in the rest of Scripture (most of them in the Ten Commandments—see Exodus 20:1-17). So it ought not to surprise the Corinthians, or anyone who knows their Bible, that behaviour like this prevents people from inheriting the kingdom.

The second notable point is that Paul puts sins we regard as very serious alongside sins which we might think of as fairly trivial. Christians (rightly) see adultery as completely unacceptable, but we might be more inclined to accept greed or slander. Paul lumps them all together.

> Paul puts sins we regard as very serious alongside sins which we might think of as fairly trivial.

The third point is beautiful: "Such were some of you. But..." (1 Corinthians **6:11**, ESV). Even when listing the most grievous sins he can think of, Paul cannot stop himself from tacking back to the grace of God and the transforming work of Jesus. *This list,* he reminds them (and us!), *is exactly what you were like before Jesus changed your lives. Don't let's pretend that you were textbook examples of virtue before you came to Christ. You were immoral, idolatrous, adulterous, greedy, slandering drunkards. But you were washed clean (which is probably a reference to baptism). You were made holy. You were declared righteous in the name of the Lord Jesus Christ, by the Spirit. God changed everything about you, because of his unmerited, transforming favour in Christ.*

For that reason, they and we have both the motivation and the power to repent of sinful behaviour and inherit the kingdom. The motivation is that you want to "be who you are": to bring your lifestyle in line with the reality of who you are in Christ. You want to inherit the kingdom. You want to live out what God has done in your life.

And the power comes from the gifts that God has already given to you: baptism, **justification**, **sanctification**, and the person of the Spirit. By those means God has already changed you once, even as you continue to struggle against sin as you wait for the **renewal of all things**. (In Wesley Hill's nice phrase, we are all "washed and waiting".) If you repent of your sins, no matter how serious they are, God will change you again and again, and you will inherit the kingdom that he has prepared for you.

Trinitarian Purity

The list in **verses 9-11** bridges the two halves of 1 Corinthians 6. It brings together examples of sexual sins (sexual immorality, adultery, gay sex), which will be the focus of **verses 12-20**, and the financial and legal ones which were the focus of **verses 1-8** (theft, greed, slander, swindling). So Paul's first challenge to the Corinthians' sexual behaviour—*You used to be like this yourselves, but you were washed and sanctified and justified* (**v 11**)—has come before we even find out what they are up to. When we eventually find out, we are astonished: not only that it is being done and accepted by those who profess to be Christians, but also that it is something that Paul feels the need to argue with them about. The Corinthians are visiting prostitutes.

They have their reasons. One of them is their warped idea of Christian freedom: "I have the right to do anything" (**v 12**). This is the first clear example in the letter of a Corinthian slogan, a simple line that they use which has been passed on to Paul, probably in the report he has heard from Chloe's people (1:11). Corinthian men were using this line as a justification to have sex with whomever they wanted, and their twenty-first century successors are still using equivalent arguments today. (I am a pastor, so I have heard quite a few of them. "But we love each other." "Paul didn't have a problem with extramarital sex, only with prostitution." "But my wife and I are incompatible." "But we're planning to get married.") Paul has a crisp response. As the NIV 1984 puts it, "'Everything is permissible for me'—but not everything is beneficial. 'Everything is permissible for me'—but I will not be mastered by anything." The point of Christian freedom is to be free from sin, not to sell yourself into slavery to it.

Another argument they have, which in many ways has even more striking parallels with today, emerges from their horribly cheap view of what sex actually is: "Food for the stomach and the stomach for food, and God will destroy them both" (**6:13**). When you're hungry, you eat, and then you don't feel hungry any more. It's a natural craving which is satisfied in a natural way. Some Corinthian man are arguing that sex is just the same. It's a natural way of satisfying a physical need. You're hungry, so you eat; you want sex, so you visit a prostitute. She is no more than food for a hungry man or a toilet in which to relieve himself. What's the problem with that?

The rest of the chapter sees Paul explaining the three very large problems with that, and in a remarkably theological (and **trinitarian**) way. The first problem is that our bodies are members of Christ (**v 15**). We are destined for the same resurrection as he experienced (**v 14**), and we are united with him in spirit (**v 17**). At the same time, having sex with a person is an act of one-flesh union with them, and it has been ever since Eden (**v 16**, quoting Genesis 2:24). So is it right for me to take a body that is united with Christ and unite it with a prostitute? Of course not (1 Corinthians **6:15**)!

The second problem relates to the Holy Spirit. God has given you his Spirit, and he dwells in you, which makes your body a temple, the very dwelling place of God (**v 19**). Your body, in that sense, is sacred space. And while there are all sorts of sins which take place outside the body, and as such do not defile the "temple" in the same way, sexual sin takes place inside the body, within the temple courts, and is therefore a sin "against [your] own body" (**v 18**). The Corinthians have been working hard to cheapen sex, to turn it into a bodily function like eating or urinating. Paul, unmarried himself (7:7-8), insists that it is a sacred, one-flesh-forming **mystery**, and should therefore be treated with reverence.

Paul's trinitarian case for sexual purity concludes with God the Father: "You are not your own; you were bought at a price. Therefore honour God with your bodies" (**6:19-20**). The great lie at the heart of sexual immorality, and ultimately of any form of sin, is the idea that we are our own. If I am mine, then I get to decide what to do, how to spend my time and who to sleep with. But I am not mine. I was bought by God, for the unthinkably great price of his own Son. So my sex life does not belong to me but to him, and he has made his will for me very clear: "Flee from sexual immorality" (**v 18**).

A few years ago, the American pastor Alan Noble commented that churches will only thrive in the modern world to the extent that they embrace the first line of the Heidelberg Catechism. This outstanding summary of Christian teaching, which was originally written in Germany in the 1560s, begins by asking, "What is your only comfort in life and in death?" The answer is one of the most powerful paragraphs in Christian literature, and it begins, "That I am not my own, but I belong body and soul, in life and in death, to my faithful Saviour Jesus Christ". That is Paul's point here, and it is the foundation for a life of sexual purity and Christian fidelity. I am not mine. You are not yours. Praise God.

Questions for reflection

1. Practically, what steps could you take if you had a dispute with a fellow believer—either within your church or denomination or outside of it?

2. How does Paul stir up repentance in verses 7-11? How do these verses challenge or encourage you personally?

3. Do you need to change anything about the way you think about or use your body?

PART TWO

It would be a bit of an exaggeration to say that chapters 5 – 7 were all about sex—but not much. Paul spends eight verses on lawsuits (6:1-8) and eight verses on circumcision and slavery (7:17-24). That aside, this entire section of the letter is concerned with what we might call sexual ethics: incest, sexual immorality, marriage, divorce, remarriage and singleness.

That is one of the reasons why 1 Corinthians feels so relevant to our contemporary world. In some New Testament books, the presenting issues are things which do not directly affect most of us today: **table fellowship** with Gentiles and **circumcision** in Galatians, for instance, or the perceived ongoing value of **priesthood** and animal sacrifices in Hebrews. But no one could say that about 1 Corinthians. Sex was one of the biggest issues in their culture, and it is one of the biggest issues in ours.

Roman Corinth, like the contemporary West, seems to have had a view of sex that was both too high and too low at the same time. In some ways they prized it too much, treating it as something of a god, and they needed to be taught that a **celibate** life was not just possible but actually (as we will see in chapter 7) preferable. But in other ways they prized it too little, seeing it merely as a natural bodily function, with no mystery or spirituality or transcendence. Our culture does much the same, seeing sex as everything one minute (how can you live a full life without it?) and as nothing the next (why does it even matter who we have sex with?)

History, Theology and Culture

That makes Paul's teaching here hugely valuable for us, in at least three ways. At a historical level, it reminds us of something which we easily forget: that we have been here before. Ours is not the first generation to be characterised by an obsession with sex, widespread immorality and abuse, boastfulness about sexual licence and confusion about who gets to sleep with whom. If anything, the Greco-Roman world was more messed up on this stuff than we are. The true sexual revolution, as historians like Kyle Harper have shown, was not the promiscuity that has transformed the West since the 1960s. It was the insistence on faithful **monogamy**, in a way that constrained men but liberated women, that transformed the Roman Empire through the influence of early Christianity (see *From Shame to Sin: The Christian Transformation of Sexual Morality in Late Antiquity*).

At a theological level, Paul gives us some priceless teaching that explains not only how sex should and should not be used, but why. And his reasons are not the ones that Christian young people are often given today. They are not trivial or self-interested ("If you wait until marriage, then your sex life will be better", for instance, or "You're less likely to catch a sexually transmitted infection that way"). Rather, they are unashamedly theological.

> Paul explains not only how sex should and should not be used, but why. And his reasons are unashamedly theological.

All of his reasons are connected to the big picture—to the central themes of Christian teaching. Paul connects sex to our doctrine of the church: "A little yeast leavens the whole batch of dough" (5:6). He connects it to our understanding of salvation: "You were washed, you were sanctified, you were justified" (6:11). He links it to our **anthropology**: "Your bodies are members of Christ" (v 15), and then a few verses later, "Your bodies are temples of the Holy Spirit" (v 19). He connects it to eschatology: "The time is short" (7:29). Paul is continually drawing us back to the theological reasons for Christian sexual ethics, rather than simply giving the Corinthians a list of "dos" and "don'ts". That helps us understand the restrictions God places on sex, and makes those restrictions a lot more compelling.

And at a cultural level, Paul's method here has a huge amount to teach us. For those of us who are following Jesus in the contemporary West, Christian sexual ethics look increasingly arbitrary. (I heard someone remark that God's preference for sex within heterosexual marriage, rather than sex outside of it, can look to many people like a preference for red and black jelly babies rather than green and yellow ones.) In this cultural context, it is crucial that we learn from Paul's method here and continually look to frame our teaching on sexual ethics in the context of a much bigger story about God, the world and the gospel. It is only by communicating what sex is—what it means, what it represents, what it is for—that we will be able to help people make sense of why God cares who we sleep with and why his instructions are good.

My friend Sam Allberry tells the story of a friend who has a very bizarre spoon in his sugar bowl. It is a bit larger than a teaspoon, but it has a big hole in the middle, so it is unable to carry sugar, salt, cocoa, or pretty much anything for which you would need a teaspoon. When he has people round, he enjoys watching them trying to work out how to use it and whether they are doing something wrong. Eventually he reveals that it is an olive spoon, and that it is meant to have a hole in it so that you can drain the liquid as you lift the olive to your mouth. "You can't make sense of the way the spoon is without understanding what it's for," Sam explains. And then comes the punchline: "It is true of my friend's olive spoon, and it is true of our sexuality" (*Seven Myths About Singleness*, page 105).

It's an important observation. Frequently, cultural conversations about sexual ethics take place on the basis that everyone knows what sex is for—basically, physical enjoyment and/or emotional connection—and the only disagreement is over what limits you should put on it: age, consent, the number and sex of your partner(s), whether you are related to them, whether you are married to them, and so on. Sex, so the thinking goes, is just an enjoyable physical bonding experience between two consenting adults, like tandem skydiving, only cheaper (and without clothes on). The only question is whether you're going to be bigoted about who gets to do it with whom.

But the Christian vision of sex is far deeper than that. It is not less than the contemporary view—it certainly is an enjoyable physical bonding experience between two consenting adults—but it is an awful lot more. So before we get into a debate over who gets to do what with whom, we need to do what Paul does, and ask a much deeper and richer question. What is sex for?

The Meaning of Sex

An obvious answer, and one we should not overlook, is that the primary purpose of sex is to have children. (The next few paragraphs are adapted from my chapter on sex in *God of All Things*, chapter 10.) Everything that makes it delightful—physical, emotional, hormonal, spiritual—is designed to strengthen the bond between husband and wife and enable them to face the challenges of pregnancy, birth and parenthood together. It is easy to forget this in a society where it is so common to have sex without producing children (through contraception) and to produce children without having sex (through IVF). But it is clearly foundational to what sex is for, from "be fruitful and increase in number" onwards (Genesis 1:28). Sex points towards children, biblically speaking. To make love is to give yourself up, not just to the person before you but to the little person who may come after you.

If we stand much further back, however, we notice that sex is about creation. Think for a moment about Genesis 1: the entire structure of creation is made up of **complementary** pairs, which are distinguished from one another as part of God's creative design. In the beginning, the earth is "formless and empty", and God's creative work consists of making distinctions between things, or separating things, to bring about order and life. We get light and dark, day and night, heaven and earth, land and sea, sun and moon, male and female. Sex (which until very recently just meant "male" or "female", rather than "sexual intercourse") mirrors the one-to-one harmony—the complementarity, the "fit"—that exists throughout creation.

We don't have one sun and many moons, or two days for every one night; we have one of each. We don't get life if we have earth above and earth below (which is basically what a cave is), or sky above and sky below (which is basically what a gas giant like Jupiter is); we get life through having one of each, with the sky above producing water and the earth below receiving it and bearing forth life. (I'm guessing the sexual parallels don't need a diagram.) And just as male and female are separated in creation but with a view to being united again in marriage, so the heavens and the earth, though separated for now, will ultimately be united in cosmic "marriage" in the new creation (Revelation 21:1-3). Two will become one, and those whom God has joined together, let no one separate.

Sex is also about worship. Biblically, there is a connection between the number of gods you worship and the number of sexual partners you have. The Ten Commandments demand an exclusive approach to worship ("You shall have no other gods but me", Exodus 20:3) and an exclusive approach to sexuality (effectively, *You shall have no other husbands/wives but him/her*, v 14). When Israel violated one, from the golden-calf incident onwards (Exodus 32), they usually violated the other. The book of Hosea develops this image in particularly graphic detail, picturing God as a faithful husband and Israel as his prostitute wife, but many other biblical writers present idolatry as an act of sexual immorality with other gods: "They whored after other gods and bowed down to them" (Judges 2:17, ESV). Paul makes the point that idolatry is mirrored in sexual immorality, with both involving the abandonment of one God/partner who is different from you in exchange for many gods/partners who are the same as you (Romans 1:18-27). Our sexuality reflects our worship. Faithfulness in one reflects faithfulness in the other.

And sex is about the gospel. Sexual relations shared between a husband and a wife within the context of marriage offer a profound parable of the Christian message. "Therefore a man shall leave his father and mother and hold fast to his wife," says Paul, "and the two shall become one flesh. This mystery is profound, and I am saying that it refers to Christ and the church" (Ephesians 5:31-32, ESV). We make promises, we forsake all others, we exchange rings, we celebrate with a meal, we share all our worldly possessions, we take on a new family name, and then we have sex as a physical seal of our commitment, trusting that out of it God will bring forth new life, and celebrating our union with and surrender to one another.

Each of those steps preaches the gospel. Jesus promises never to leave us or abandon us. We promise to forsake all other gods, as long as we both shall live. He gives us a gift that seals the **covenant** (his Holy Spirit) and provides a meal for us to celebrate with the whole family (bread and wine). All his possessions become ours and all our debts become his. We take on his name. We enter into union with Christ and get baptised in water as a physical seal of our commitment, trusting that out of it God will bring forth new life, and celebrating our union with and surrender to one another.

A Signpost

Sex is a beautiful thing—a loving gift from a bountiful and abundant God. But it is not an ultimate thing. It is a shadow, a parable, a silhouette whose true fulfilment is found in the love that God has for his people. It is a signpost to another reality, and it is this that makes it mysterious, meaningful and transcendent.

Many find it surprising when they discover how much of our richest teaching on sexuality, marriage and the new creation comes from single people. John, the friend of the bridegroom; Paul, the best man; Jesus himself; and countless priests, popes, monks, nuns and other single believers spent decades reflecting on, praying for and anticipating the wedding of Christ and the church.

In many ways, however, it is not surprising at all. Married people, when they assume that sex is ultimately there for them and their spouse, can get so preoccupied with the picture that they forget the ultimate reality, like someone at the Victoria Falls watching video footage of it on their phone. Single people often know better. Sex is a signpost. It is but a glimpse of a relationship, a union and a happiness that are grander and deeper than our wildest imagining. "Blessed are those who are invited to the wedding supper of the Lamb!" (Revelation 19:9).

Questions for reflection

1. What arguments have you heard people give for and against sex outside heterosexual marriage? What do those arguments assume about what sex is for?

2. To what extent does your own experience of sex (or your experience of the way others talk about or portray sex) match the three meanings outlined above?

3. How would you explain the Christian view of sex to an unbelieving friend?

5. MARRIAGE AND SINGLENESS

Whenever I am trying to show someone how difficult it is to translate the Bible, I go to 1 Corinthians **7:1**. In the NIV, it looks fairly straightforward; the Corinthians have obviously written to Paul saying, "It is good for a man not to have sexual relations with a woman". But this translation involves three major decisions. The first is the decision to present this statement as a quotation from the Corinthians' letter rather than as Paul's own view; there are no quotation marks in the Greek original. The second is to take it as a statement ("It is good...") rather than a question ("Is it good...?") The third is to translate *hapto* as "have sexual relations with" when in most normal circumstances it simply means "touch." To an English reader, those things sound remarkably different.

I happen to think the NIV has got all three decisions right. But English translations vary dramatically. The King James Version renders it literally and leaves the reader to work out how to apply it: "It is good for a man not to touch a woman". The Good News Bible goes for "A man does well not to marry". The International Standard Version takes it as a question: "Is it advisable for a man not to touch a woman inappropriately?" In the Christian Standard Bible it is a statement, but in one of two alternative options given in a footnote the verb has a different meaning again: "It is good for a man not to use a woman for sex". How do we sort through this tangle?

To begin with, it is likely that the phrase is a quotation from the Corinthians' letter to Paul rather than Paul's own view. One of the distinctive things about 1 Corinthians is the number of times Paul appears to quote the church and then correct their view (something we saw happen several times in chapter 6, for instance). Here, for the first time, Paul makes it explicit that he is replying to their letter ("the matters you wrote about") rather than the news he has received from Chloe's people. So it seems natural that he would quote them and respond accordingly.

In some ways it matters less whether we see the quotation as a statement ("It is good…") or a question ("Is it good…?") It would be interesting to know, of course, and it would tell us something about the Corinthians; it would give us a sense of whether they were agreed on the subject or whether they were asking Paul to adjudicate a debate they were having. But it does not affect our interpretation of the rest of the chapter that much, for the simple reason that we are primarily dealing with Paul's view rather than theirs. I tend to take it as a statement, but Paul's argument makes equally good sense if it is a question.

The big challenge with translating the verse, and the reason for such different outcomes, is that we are dealing with an idiom and a euphemism. The word "touch" in Greek functioned a bit like "sleep with" does in English; we all know that it refers to having sex, even though the words literally mean something else. As a result, most translations opt for some variation on "have sexual relations with", because they are trying to communicate the English equivalent of the Greek phrase rather than its dictionary definition. Personally I think that is the best approach here.

But it is also possible that the phrase is more negative than that. A number of scholars, based on other appearances of the verb in ancient Greek, think it refers not just to having sex but to the use of a woman for sexual gratification (which, as we already know from chapter 6, was a significant problem in the church). Roy Ciampa and Brian Rosner's excellent commentary offers a contemporary version: "It is good for a man not to bed / bang / shag a woman" (*The First Letter to the Corinthians*, page 275). My own view is that Paul's response in the subsequent verses makes more sense if the question is about the legitimacy of having sexual relations at all rather than the more self-gratifying (or even abusive) version. But either way, we are less interested in their confusion than in Paul's clarity, which now follows.

Walking a Tightrope

One of the great challenges facing the contemporary church, half a century on from the so-called "sexual revolution" of the 1960s and 1970s, is how to speak and think about sex. Christianity has an incomparably high view of sex within marriage, as we see from Genesis onwards, but most poetically and erotically in the Song of Songs. It also has an incomparably high view of celibate singleness, as reflected in the life of Jesus himself and many others (including, as we are about to discover, Paul). The question is: how do we champion singleness— in a culture where it is increasingly looked down upon—without being ascetic, anti-sex and anti-marriage? And how do we champion sex within marriage—in a culture where it is increasingly under attack from all sides—without disparaging singleness?

Walking this tightrope is made more complicated by the fact that the church is always communicating to two different audiences. Outside the church the Christian insistence on sex within marriage, for reasons that we considered in the previous chapter, is regarded as quaint at best and actively harmful at worst. So when we are communicating to society as a whole, we want to prize and explain our high view of sexual intimacy within marriage. But inside the church the challenge is often the reverse: there is often an obsession with marriage, in which the nuclear family is normalised, married life is idolised, and single people are marginalised. So when we are talking to the family of God, we want to insist on the goodness of the single life and the crucial reality that we are not made complete in marriage or sexual fulfilment but in Jesus. Addressing the first problem risks making the second problem worse, and vice versa. How can we handle the subject wisely?

By learning from Paul. In the **providence** of God, not only was our Saviour unmarried—and we could probably do with reflecting as much on the virginity of Jesus as we do on the virginity of Mary—but so was the apostle to the Gentiles. That is a gift to all of us. The person responsible for writing the vast majority of what the New Testament teaches about sex and marriage was single himself (and the same is true for many of the church's greatest teachers on the subject), so his teaching cannot be dismissed as self-interested or unrealistic. Paul, like Jesus, walked the walk on this one.

Paul begins his response to the Corinthians' quotation by affirming the goodness of sex within marriage. It might be tempting when faced with the sort of sexual antics occurring in this particular church to try to ban sex altogether (as some religious sects have in the past, although for obvious reasons they don't tend to last very long). Paul does the opposite. The best defence against sexual immorality, he says, is for all married people to have sexual relations with their husbands or wives (**7:2**). A married person has a "marital duty" to their spouse (**v 3**)—an obligation to serve the other person with their body. He goes further: married couples should not deprive themselves of sexual intimacy, and if they do, they should only do so for a short while so that they can pray, and then quickly come back together so that they may not be tempted (**v 5**).

This is a remarkably "sex positive" paragraph, and Paul (as ever) has a theological rationale for it (**v 4**): "The wife does not have authority over her own body but yields it to her husband," he explains. This statement would presumably have gone down well with the men in the church, and with most men in the ancient world as well as plenty in the modern one; when she gets married, a woman yields authority over her body to her husband. But his next line is a game-changer: "In the same way, the husband does not have authority over his own body but yields it to his wife". Greek men certainly did not believe that their wives had authority over their bodies. It would have sounded absurd to them. But Paul is adamant: marriage is not one-sided. It requires just as much self-yielding from a man as it requires from a woman. Sexual relations—like marriage as a whole—only work properly when both partners yield to the other, preferring the other to themselves and looking to serve them in any way they can.

It sounds like an ancient sex manual. Making love is good, and husbands and wives should enjoy it frequently; they should give themselves up to each other, and they should not abstain except for a very short time. And then comes the kicker: "I say this as a concession, not as a command. I wish that all of you were as I am. But each of you has your own gift from God; one has this gift, another has that" (**v 6-7**). Suddenly and without warning, Paul has gone from extolling the value of marital sex to putting it firmly in its place. *I am conceding all this rather than commanding it,* he says.

If I had my way, everyone would be single like me. But to be fair, we all have different gifts. You have yours, and I have mine.

Paul's statement on singleness is so counter-cultural that it stops us in our tracks.

This comment is so counter-cultural, both then and now, that it stops us in our tracks. Paul seems to be saying—shock horror!—that he thinks the single life is preferable to the married one, although he is happy to admit that we all have different gifts, so they can both be good. It is an astonishing remark that will be spelled out at more length, and in fact reinforced, later on (**v 8-9**, 25-38). For now, it is worth noticing the nuance and wisdom with which Paul handles the challenge we mentioned earlier. How do we walk the tightrope of affirming the goodness of sex within marriage, yet at the same time affirming the goodness of the celibate single life? Like this. (Though I would also recommend reading and applying Sam Allberry's excellent book *Seven Myths About Singleness*.)

Good, Right, Beautiful

Paul has just dropped a bit of a bombshell, so he quickly explains what he thinks that means for those who are not married. "Now to the unmarried and the widows I say: it is good for them to stay unmarried, as I do" (**v 8**). If we were wondering whether Paul's previous comment was a bit whimsical, rather than a genuine conviction about the goodness of the unmarried life, this sets us straight. Remaining unmarried, whether we have never got married or whether our spouse has died, is *kalos*: good, right, beautiful. That's what Paul has done, and it's what he recommends for single people everywhere. If we struggle to recommend the single life and to affirm it as good, right and beautiful, then it might be worth reflecting on why, and on what Paul knows that we don't. He will help us on this later in the chapter (v 25-38).

This verse raises the question of whether Paul was ever married. Was he always single? Did his wife die? Did his wife leave him, perhaps because he became a Christian? We will never know for sure, although I am inclined to think that he was always single; if he had experienced either bereavement or abandonment, we might expect him to have mentioned it when addressing those specific situations in this chapter (v 12-16, 39-40). In the present context, however, it does not really matter. The point is that he regards his own experience of being unmarried as an example for people to imitate rather than a curse for people to escape.

Having said that, Paul is not banning marriage either. "But if they cannot control themselves, they should marry, for it is better to marry than to burn with passion" (**v 9**). Marriage might not be his preference, but it is far better than remaining single and being consumed with sexual passion, leading to a lack of self-control and sexual immorality. Once again, the pastoral wisdom and nuance with which Paul handles the various possibilities are exemplary for all of us.

Questions for reflection

1. Is it in any way true in your church that marriage is idolised and single people are marginalised? What could you do to redress the balance on this?

2. If you're married, does your sex life follow Paul's instructions? How could you and your spouse serve each other better in this area?

3. How does this passage alter what you might say to your single friends or unmarried children about their future?

PART TWO

Divorce and Remarriage

I have never owned a Bible with red letters. I don't object to them, and I can see why people use them; I've just never had one myself. It seems to me that you either have a Bible where all the words of Jesus are in red or you have a Bible where all the words of God are in black. Somewhere, deep down, I think I've probably also been suspicious of the implications: that if the words of Jesus are more important, then that makes the words of **Moses** or **David** or Paul somehow less important and therefore liable to be relativised or even dismissed.

In his teaching on divorce and remarriage, Paul shows me a better way forward. The teaching of the Lord Jesus is, and should be, the most important teaching we have anywhere. Paul is very aware of which situations Jesus addressed during his earthly ministry ("not I, but the Lord", **v 10**), and which situations he didn't ("I, not the Lord", **v 12**). If we have a word from Jesus, that settles the discussion. But that does not mean that we are left guessing what to believe if we don't. Paul was commissioned by the risen Christ and given the Spirit of God (**v 40**), which enabled him to teach with authority into the wide range of situations which Jesus did not comment on directly—in this case, the sticky pastoral questions around divorce and remarriage.

The teaching of Jesus is clear, Paul says: "A wife must not separate from her husband. But if she does, she must remain unmarried or else be reconciled to her husband. And a husband must not divorce his wife" (**v 10-11**). Jesus was uncompromising in his teaching on divorce and remarriage, in a way that makes many of us uncomfortable (see Matthew 5:31-32; 19:3-12; Mark 10:2-12; Luke 16:18), and this is Paul's summary of it. Disciples who are married should not separate. If they do, they should not get divorced but either remain separated or be reconciled to each other. Jesus makes an exception in the case of those who are the victims of sexual immorality, but otherwise this is a pretty emphatic "no" to divorce and remarriage.

But Jesus said nothing about disciples whose spouses are unbelievers. Should they stay married as well? What if the unbelieving partner doesn't want to, and simply abandons the marriage—what should the Christian spouse do then? Paul, aware that Jesus did not address this situation but that some Corinthians have encountered it, gives his considered response. He takes the two scenarios in turn.

First, if the unbelieving partner wants to remain married, then that's what the believing spouse should do, whether they are the husband or the wife (1 Corinthians **7:12-13**; once again, Paul extends privileges and responsibilities to women that would usually have only belonged to men). Being married to a believer has a sanctifying effect on a person, on the home, and on any children they may have (**v 14**). It exposes them to holiness and to the truth of the gospel in ways that would not be true if the Christian separated from their spouse. Paul is not saying that people are automatically saved by being married to or parented by a Christian; he says we have no way of knowing that (**v 16**). But he seems to believe that it makes their salvation far more likely in the end and their life far more "holy" in the meantime.

Second, if the unbelieving partner wants to separate, then "let it be so. The brother or the sister is not bound in such circumstances; God has called us to live in peace" (**v 15**). At first glance this seems simple enough. If you are married to an unbeliever and they want to separate, you should let them go rather than trying to enforce the marriage, because God has called us to peace. But then the question immediately arises: can such a person—a Christian whose unbelieving spouse has left them—get married again to someone else?

It all comes down to the meaning of the phrase "not bound" (or "not enslaved", ESV). Some interpreters argue that this refers to being freed from marriage and the obligation to maintain it when your partner clearly does not want to. Others argue it refers to being free to remarry, on the basis that a legitimate divorce would make possible a legitimate remarriage. It is difficult to settle a complex question on the basis of just two Greek words, although my own view inclines towards the latter.

Paul's brief treatment here leaves all sorts of questions unanswered. What if I got divorced illegitimately but now my ex-spouse has died? What if I was divorced before I was converted? What about domestic abuse? What if I was divorced for bad reasons but now I have a new partner and we have children together? The list of scenarios is endless, and often painful, and this is not the place to go into them all in detail. Nevertheless, here are five principles that might be helpful.

The first two are for those of us in complicated situations who are looking for godly wisdom on our future relationships:

1. If in doubt, stay unmarried. This is Paul's counsel to all of us in this chapter, not just those who have been divorced.

2. Submit to local church leadership. Your pastors are not perfect, but they have been given to you by God to help with exactly these sort of situations, and their distance from a situation should enable them to see the best way forward more clearly than those who are directly involved.

The next three principles are for pastors:

3. Distinguish between short-term solutions and long-term commitments. If someone is in danger in their home, they should be protected immediately, by separating from their partner and informing law enforcement, whether or not they are subsequently advised or allowed to get divorced and remarried.

4. Draw wisdom from the **Reformers**. The **Protestant Reformation** of the sixteenth and seventeenth centuries produced a number of outstanding treatments of this subject, which steer a middle course between the total ban on divorce that we find in Roman Catholicism and the permissive soup of post-1960s Western culture (including Western church culture). Thomas Cranmer, who wrote the marriage vows that many of us use, identified five grounds for divorce and remarriage—adultery, desertion with malice, prolonged absence without news, deadly hostility and ill-treatment—which basically amount to the three "a"s: adultery,

abandonment and abuse. Chapter 24 of the **Westminster Confession of Faith** gives a remarkable summary of the **Presbyterian** position in less than 400 words. Wisdom like this from previous centuries can really help us.

5. If possible, write a paper that makes your church's position as clear as possible, so that members can see how you handle the issue and why. Marriage breakdown is hard enough to handle without facing complete confusion on what happens next.

Remain As You Are

The central section of the chapter provides a rationale both for what comes before it (instructions on divorce and remarriage) and for what comes after it (those who are currently unmarried). The key principle is obviously important to Paul because he states it three times in only eight verses, with only slight variations: "Each person should live as a believer in whatever situation the Lord has assigned to them, just as God has called them. This is the rule I lay down in all the churches" (**v 17**; see also **v 20, 24**).

At face value, that looks like a statement that a person's situation in life should not change from the moment they become a Christian. Is Paul saying that Christians should not change jobs? Get married? Accept promotions? Move house? Some **commentators** have taken it this way, on the basis that Paul expected the return of Christ at any moment (**v 29-31**). But there are two reasons to suggest that he is doing something subtler than that.

The first is Paul's own story. Clearly, the transformation in Paul's life when he met the risen Christ was not simply "spiritual" but related to his physical situation and his circumstances. His work, if we can call it that, completely changed. So did his relationships. So did his physical location. It would be very strange if Paul, of all people, were to teach that conversion should make no difference to what we do and where we do it.

The second is found in the examples he gives by way of explanation. Take circumcision (**v 18-20**): nobody who is uncircumcised should get circumcised, and nobody who is circumcised should try to reverse it. Paul starts with that example partly because the Corinthians would presumably have thought it was obvious, even if Jewish church members might have been taken aback by the stark announcement that "circumcision is nothing and uncircumcision is nothing" (**v 19**). But if we know Paul, and particularly his letter to the Galatians, we also know that circumcision is his go-to example of how human beings pursue righteousness in the sight of God and others. So by using circumcision as his example here, Paul is highlighting the fact that none of the things we do—getting married, staying single, getting circumcised, staying uncircumcised—add anything to our standing before God. In that sense, they are "nothing". So if you are getting married or staying unmarried for that reason, forget it. Marriage is nothing and singleness is nothing; "Keeping God's commands is what counts".

> None of the things we do add anything to our standing before God. In that sense, they are "nothing".

Or consider slavery. If you came to Christ as a slave, "don't let it trouble you" (1 Corinthians **7:21**). In a world where slavery was completely normal and where runaway slaves were executed, Paul knew that many of his converts would be enslaved for life, and he wanted them not to be troubled by that; after all, slaves are free people in Christ, just as free people are slaves in Christ (**v 22**). Having said that, the opportunity of freedom may present itself, and if it does, Christians should take it: "If you can gain your freedom, do so" (**v 21**).

This, too, is remarkably helpful when it comes to marriage and singleness. If you are unmarried and you don't want to be, it may be helpful to insert yourself into **verses 21-24**. If the opportunity to be married presents itself, you should take it. If it doesn't, don't let it trouble you; the person who is single at conversion is married to the Lord. And whether you get married or not, you must not regard yourself as owned by anyone except Christ: "You were bought at a price; do not become slaves of human beings" (**v 23**).

Single-minded

When it comes to singleness—**verses 25-40** address both single women (*parthenoi*, "virgins") and unmarried men (*agamoi*)—we are once again dealing with a subject that Jesus did not address in his earthly ministry. Paul cannot appeal to a quotation from the Gospels. What he can do is to "give a judgment as one who by the Lord's mercy is trustworthy" (**v 25**). That judgment is clear and has been expounded at some length in the previous section: "I think that it is good for a man to remain as he is" (**v 26**).

It is almost embarrassingly straightforward. If you are engaged, don't try and get out of it. If you are not, don't try and get married (**v 27**). Marriage is certainly not sinful, and Paul is very clear about that, but he is also aware that marriage presents all sorts of difficulties in this life which, in his view, are best avoided (**v 28**). Some scholars argue that there were particular circumstances in Corinth which make this true—a famine, a wave of persecution, or some other social upheaval—on the basis of the phrase "because of the present crisis" (**v 26**). Personally, I think we get closer to Paul's meaning if we understand the word *ananke* not as a "crisis", which implies an intense short-term problem, but rather as a present "necessity" or "constraint". Read this way, Paul's advice to "remain as you are" is based not on an unusually terrible situation but simply on the challenges of life in this fallen world.

That is certainly how he explains himself in his next sentence: "What I mean, brothers and sisters, is that the time is short" (**v 29**). Paul is well-known (and occasionally ridiculed) for living his life in anticipation of the return of Christ, just as Jesus taught his disciples to. But he could hardly look less like a **cult** member or crazed survivalist. He does not respond by hoarding things or stockpiling supplies or moving to Israel or building underground bunkers. He simply urges that people not hold on too tightly to the things of this world: marriage (**v 29**), the emotional ups and downs of circumstances, and purchases and possessions (**v 30-31**). None of those things are bad in themselves. But all of them can trick us into thinking we will have them for ever. We won't—and we need to live accordingly, "for this world in its present form is passing away" (**v 31**).

That, in a nutshell, is Paul's case for singleness based on the future. In the next paragraph, he makes a different argument, advocating singleness on the basis of what we could call focus. Unmarried people, Paul explains, can be exclusively devoted to what the Lord wants them to do (**v 32, 34**). They can be single-minded. If God calls them to a dangerous and possibly life-threatening mission—as happened to Paul himself—they can drop everything and go. But married people, rightly, are "concerned about the affairs of this world", in that they have to think of their spouse and their children (**v 33-34**). So if our goal is "undivided devotion to the Lord" (**v 35**), then remaining single is clearly preferable to marriage.

These are compelling reasons. But alongside a commitment to the disciple's future and the disciple's focus, Paul also insists on the disciple's freedom: their liberty of conscience when it comes to any decision which is not sinful. Few decisions prompt such soul-searching as the decision to get married. Few questions generate the search for God-given signs or divine confirmation like that of whether so-and-so is "the one". Paul, however, is cheerfully relaxed about the whole thing. Getting married to your fiancé(e) isn't sinful. If you want to get married, you should (**v 36**). On the other hand, if you have resolved not to get married, that's the right decision too (**v 37**).

Paul, true to form, thinks that marriage is good but singleness is even better (**v 38**) and that people are happier if they stay as they are (**v 40**). But he cares more about Christian freedom than he does about believers remaining single. A follower of Jesus has the freedom to marry whomever they like, whether they are single (**v 36**) or widowed (**v 39**). The only requirement is that their chosen partner "must belong to the Lord".

Questions for reflection

1. In what ways does this chapter challenge your pre-existing views about marriage and singleness? What will you say, pray or do differently as a result?

2. Do you know people in complex marital situations (perhaps you are in one yourself)? What hope does this passage give?

3. Is there anything in your life that you wish were different but you cannot change? How could focusing on keeping God's commands help you to be at peace about that?

6. LAYING DOWN YOUR RIGHTS

At the beginning of 1 Corinthians 7, Paul turned his attention from addressing the discouraging oral reports he had heard about the church—of pride, division, litigation and sexual immorality—towards the topics the Corinthians had raised in their letter to him. They had apparently written to Paul with at least six specific questions, and Paul responds to each of them in turn, beginning each answer with the phrase "Now about..." (7:25; **8:1**; 12:1; 16:1, 12) or "Now for..." (7:1). The first two questions, on marriage and singleness, seem very familiar to us. The third one, on idol food, probably doesn't.

But in many parts of the world today, it would be a familiar issue for believers. Food raises enormous questions in many cultures, particularly those where the local religion imposes dietary restrictions. A friend of mine tells of how, after a whole day's teaching in Pakistan on these very chapters, he asked if there were any questions, and the first response was "Can a Christian eat eels?" In the West, however, although we may occasionally wonder about halal meat, issues like this are not uppermost in our minds.

In the first century, this was a live issue. Most New Testament books address the subject of food in some form, and in several of them—Acts, Galatians and this letter, for instance—food plays an absolutely pivotal role. Could Christians eat meat? Could Christians eat meat that the Old Testament law prohibited as unclean? Could Jewish Christians eat with Gentile Christians? Could Christians eat food that had been sacrificed to idols? Could they do so if the meal was in a pagan temple? If it was sold in the meat market? If it was eaten in a private home? If nobody else was watching? Why?

So, before getting into Paul's response, which will occupy us for the next three chapters, we need to establish exactly what he is talking about here and what he is not. Some readers, noticing similarities with Romans 14 – 15, think he is talking about whether disciples can eat meat at all. He isn't. Others, more familiar with Acts or Galatians, might assume he is talking about the Jewish food laws. He isn't. He is talking about *eidolothuta*: idol food, or as the NIV translates it, "food sacrificed to idols" (1 Corinthians **8:1**). In Roman Corinth, as in much of the Mediterranean, pagan worship often involved the slaughtering of sacrificial animals, which would then either be eaten in a temple dining room, often as part of a pagan rite of worship, or sold in the meat market for ordinary people to buy and cook at home. The Corinthians were asking Paul, *Can we eat it?*

Paul's answer—and this is what can make chapters 8 – 10 somewhat confusing—is that it depends. If idol food is eaten in the context of idolatrous worship in a pagan temple, then no (8:1 – 10:22). If it is bought in the meat market without knowing where it comes from, then yes (10:25-26). If it is eaten in a private home, then yes, unless it will harm the conscience of anyone present, in which case no (10:27 – 11:1). The food itself, in other words, is not the issue; the issue is the character and context of the meal taking place. In the scholar Ben Witherington III's neat phrase, it is more about venue than menu (*The Acts of the Apostles*, page 466).

As we can see from the relative size of these three passages, Paul spends far more time on the first question (sacrificial food eaten as part of idolatrous worship in pagan temples) than on the other two. His answer—in a word, no—takes him the best part of three chapters to explain and involves a whole range of theological, social and practical considerations. We can assume from this that it was the main thrust of the Corinthians' question. We can also assume that at least some of them were pretty convinced that the answer was yes. Paul disagrees, and he wants them to understand why.

One God, One Lord

The Corinthians were divided (1:10), as we know. On a number of issues, and this is clearly one of them, we have (at least) one group urging everyone else not to eat idol food and (at least) one group insisting that there is no problem with it. The argument of the second group, as best as we can tell, is that "we all possess knowledge" (**8:1**), including the knowledge that "an idol is nothing at all in the world" and that "there is no God but one" (**v 4**). So if idols don't really exist, because there is only one God, how can eating idol food mean anything at all?

It sounds like a strong argument. It makes the pro-idol-food "knowers" look like good **monotheists**, and the anti-idol-food "weak" look like **polytheistic** weirdos who have somehow forgotten that idols aren't real. What is more, if we have read Romans 14 (which, although it was written later than 1 Corinthians, appears before it in our Bibles, and as a letter is generally better-known and more popular), we may be expecting Paul to side with the "knowers". But he doesn't. And over the next three chapters he will give two crucial reasons for this, one based on love of neighbour (chapters 8 – 9) and the other based on love of God (chapter 10).

Here is Paul's answer: yes, we are all "knowers". (Knowledge, *gnosis*, seems to have been

> Knowing things can make our egos and heads bigger; loving people can make our brothers and sisters bigger.

something of a Corinthian obsession and appears more in this letter than in any New Testament book; Paul first mentioned it in 1:5.) Fair enough. "But knowledge puffs up while love builds up" (**8:1**). Knowing things can make our egos and heads bigger; loving people can make our brothers and sisters bigger. So if you're obsessed with "knowing", then you may not know anything at all. Loving God, on the other hand, means that you end up with the best sort of "knowing" there is: being known by God (**v 2-3**).

But yes, idols don't really exist (**v 4**). There is only one God. Even if so-called "gods" do exist in some sense—there are, after all, a great many "gods" and "lords" around, and when you worship a "god", it functions as your master, even if it doesn't really exist—we don't worship them (**v 5**). For us, there is only one God and one Lord. (We'll return to this magnificent sentence in a moment.)

The problem is that not everybody "knows" this. Some people, having lived their entire lives surrounded by idols, still associate the sacrificial food with the god to whom it has been offered. (Converted Muslims and Hindus, in my experience, are usually more careful than other people to avoid the trappings of their former religion, not less, because they are more aware than most of the damage it can do.) Their consciences are more sensitive to what is happening, and they experience idol food as defiled (**v 7**). Given this, and given the fact that food doesn't actually bring us any closer to God—abstaining doesn't hinder us, and eating doesn't help us—we should be very careful about flaunting our right to eat what we like (**v 8**).

For many of us, as I have said, this can seem like a slightly remote discussion. But we should be grateful for it because it provokes Paul to give us perhaps the most extraordinary statement of the divinity of Jesus Christ in all of Scripture (with the possible exception of John 1:1), and certainly the earliest from a historical point of view: "For us there is but one God, the Father, from whom all things came and for whom we live; and there is but one Lord, Jesus Christ, through whom all things came and through whom we live" (1 Corinthians **8:6**).

The reason this text is extraordinary, as many scholars have shown, is that Paul has adapted his statement from the *Shema*, the central Jewish statement of faith in one God: "Hear, O Israel: the LORD our God, the Lord is one. Love the LORD your God with all your heart and with all your soul and with all your strength" (Deuteronomy 6:4-5).

In the history of Judaism, there is no stronger statement of monothe-
ism—of the uniqueness and exclusivity of Israel's God—than this. Yet
here is Paul, a Jewish man, quoting the most central Jewish text of all
and inserting Jesus Christ right into the middle of it. There is one God
(the Father) and one Lord (Jesus Christ). Everything comes from the
Father, and it comes through Christ. We live for the Father, and we live
through Christ. It is hard to imagine a more dramatic statement of the
supremacy, transcendence and deity of the Lord Jesus, or a more compelling reason to worship him with all our heart, soul and strength.

Rights and Wrongs

We can probably tell what Paul's punchline is going to be, but here
it comes nevertheless: "Be careful, however, that the exercise of your
rights does not become a stumbling-block to the weak" (1 Corinthians
8:9). This, in a sentence, is the point Paul is going to press home
throughout 1 Corinthians 9, using himself as an extended example.
The Corinthians may or may not have the right to eat idol food—and
this is a question to which he will return in chapter 10—but what they
absolutely must not do is to exercise their "right" in such a way as to
destroy their weaker brother or sister. It is that serious. Their dinner
has the capacity to be a *proskomma*: a stumbling-block, a trigger for
apostasy, that could scupper the faith of a fellow believer.

It works like this. Imagine one of the "weak" sees one of the
"knowers" lounging around in a pagan temple dining room, enjoying
a sacrificial piece of meat in the context of an idolatrous meal. What
might they conclude? They might conclude that they should eat idol
food as well (**8:10**). And since, for them, eating idol food is an act of
worship, they might also conclude that idolatry is compatible with
Christianity—that they can both follow Jesus and continue to serve
the pagan gods they left behind. So for the sake of a nice meal out,
the "knowing" of the "knower" has destroyed the weaker believer's
faith (**v 11**). The "knower" is sinning against them, and in doing so,
they are sinning against Christ (**v 12**).

We can all probably think of other examples. Drinking alcohol in the presence of certain individuals might cause them not just to fall off the wagon but to abandon Christianity. The food we eat, the way we spend our money, the language we use, the shows and movies we watch and even the clothes we wear have the capacity to lead others away from Christ by tempting them to violate their consciences. The language Paul uses is extremely strong here—*apollumi* (destroy), *tupto* (strike, wound), *skandalizo* (ensnare, cause to fall)—reflecting the fact that he is not just talking about giving people a difficult choice, but threatening their faith. Faced with consequences like that, my "rights" fade into insignificance: "Therefore, if what I eat causes my brother or sister to fall into sin, I will never eat meat again" (**v 13**).

What is fascinating about Paul's argument here is that he makes it at all. We have been talking so far as if "eating in an idol's temple" (**v 10**) is morally neutral, like drinking alcohol or eating meat or wearing particular clothes, and as though the only reason to abstain from it is to avoid upsetting the faith of others. We will discover later, however, that Paul does not think of it as morally neutral at all, but as fundamentally idolatrous (10:1-22). So why not say so immediately? Why make two arguments—one based on love of neighbour (chapters 8 – 9) and one based on love of God (chapter 10)—when he could have used one?

There are probably several reasons. Partly, Paul is planting the seed of an idea that will come to full flowering later: namely that love trumps freedom (see especially 1 Corinthians 13). Partly, he is making the softer argument first (put your care for others before your own rights), before ramping up to the more confrontational one later (you're actually worshipping idols). And partly, he is about to use that argument as an opportunity to respond to some of the criticisms the Corinthians have made of his own ministry, in which he has renounced his "rights" in order to serve other people. That point comes into sharp focus in 1 Corinthians 9.

Questions for reflection

1. In what situations could a focus on knowledge, facts or rights squeeze out love?

2. Pause to reflect on verse 6. What will you do or say in response to this statement?

3. Are there any "rights" you are holding on to which could upset the faith of others by tempting them to violate their consciences? What needs to change?

PART TWO

Paul's Rights

The purpose of chapter 9 has been understood in two contrasting ways. Many have read it as a digression within Paul's argument, modelled on a legal defence, in which he explains his practice of not accepting money for his ministry among the Corinthians. Advocates of this view point out that the word *apologia*—"defence"—appears near the start (**9:3**); that his refusal to be paid for preaching the gospel occupies most of the chapter (**v 1-18**); and that idol food isn't even mentioned. Others see Paul not as offering a defence, using a legal mode of writing, but offering himself as an example, using a persuasive mode of writing. (In technical language, this is known as deliberative rhetoric, as opposed to juridical rhetoric.) They argue that Paul's life is a real-life example of the principle he was teaching in 8:9-13.

> Serving our brothers and sisters matters more than our "rights". Love trumps freedom.

I think this second view is correct. Paul is presenting his model of ministry—offering the gospel free of charge, despite the theological and practical reasons why he could accept payment if he wanted to—as a real-life illustration of what he was saying in 8:9-13: namely, that believers should renounce their rights if it will help other believers. Serving our brothers and sisters matters more than our "rights" to do this or that. Love trumps freedom. Chapter 9, in that sense, is an extended explanation of why the Corinthians should not eat idol food, based on Paul's apostolic ministry.

To make this case, he begins by explaining why he has rights in the first place. He is free. He is an apostle. He has seen the risen Jesus and established the Corinthian church (**9:1**). Even if others were to dispute Paul's apostleship, the Corinthians cannot, because their very existence is evidence of it (**v 2**). So if anyone has the right to financial support—to receiving food and drink (**v 4**), to being allowed to travel with a wife like the other apostles do (**v 5**) and to refraining from paid work so that they can preach the gospel full time (**v 6**)—it is Paul.

(The mention of Barnabas here is interesting. Sometimes the case is made, from **9:1** and 15:8-9, that to be an "apostle" you had to have seen the resurrected Lord Jesus in person. This was certainly necessary for a person to join the Twelve—see Acts 1:21-22—and Paul sees it as a crucial reason for his apostolic credentials, as we have just seen. But there were plenty of people who saw the risen Christ who were not designated "apostles", and there were several "apostles"—this letter mentions Barnabas and Apollos—who, as far as we know, did not see the risen Christ. Apostleship was a slightly more open category than we have sometimes imagined.)

Therefore, Paul has the "right" to receive income for preaching the gospel. There are obvious human parallels. Soldiers don't work for free, and nor do farmers and nor do shepherds (1 Corinthians **9:7**). These examples are not random but rather reflect Paul's view of apostolic ministry as work in which you have to fight, plant seeds, plough fields and look after sheep (compare 2 Timothy 2:3-7). If all these people don't work for free, then why should gospel workers have to?

We can go beyond human examples into the Old Testament law itself (1 Corinthians **9:8**). Moses himself said, "Do not muzzle an ox while it is treading out the grain" (**v 9**, quoting Deuteronomy 25:4). And when he did, he wasn't just talking about oxen; he was talking about the principle that ploughing and threshing should be rewarded with a share in the harvest (1 Corinthians **9:10**). *We have sown spiritually among you, by preaching the gospel,* Paul points out: *Surely, then, we have the right to reap materially—as other people do, even if we don't (**v 12**)—by receiving financial support from you (**v 11**).* It's a first-century equivalent of "The Little Red Hen".

So Paul has the right to be paid for preaching the gospel. It's clear from human **analogies** (**v 7**). It's clear from the law (**v 8-11**), which incidentally also mandates that "those who serve in the temple get their food from the temple" (**v 13**). It is even clear from the teaching of Jesus himself, when he sent out the apostles and said that "the worker deserves his wages" (Luke 10:7). So there should be no question about whether or not Paul has the right to receive payment for preaching. "The Lord has commanded that those who preach the gospel should receive their living from the gospel" (1 Corinthians **9:14**).

Paul's Refusal

Paul's point has been a long time in coming, but now it finally arrives: "But I have not used any of these rights" (**v 15**). *I am entitled to receive money from you for preaching the gospel, but I have laid my "rights" to one side in order to serve you as effectively as possible.* Paul isn't using a piece of **reverse psychology** here, in the hope that they will start funding him after all this time (**v 16**). He is pointing out how his own apostolic practice—supporting himself by working as a tentmaker rather than receiving payment (Acts 18:3)—embodies the point he is making about idol food. Love for others is more important than your right to eat whatever you want or earn whatever you think you deserve.

Paul's refusal to accept payment for preaching is surprising for several reasons and deserves a moment's reflection. As he has been at pains to show, it conflicts with the clear teaching of both the law (1 Corinthians **9:8-11**) and the Lord (**v 14**). It is out of step with what virtually all the other apostles do (**v 3-6**). Even more strangely, it is different from what he tells other people to do; he teaches that elders who preach and teach should be paid (1 Timothy 5:17-18), based on the exact same teachings from Moses and Jesus. So why does he refuse payment himself? And should pastors and churches today take their cues from what he said or from what he did?

To take the second question first, it seems clear that Paul wanted his churches to follow his teaching rather than his example. Usually, as he explains in 1 Timothy, the elders or pastors who preach and teach should be materially rewarded (although this is not the same thing as saying they should be paid a full-time salary; Paul never says that, and in many parts of the world today that would be totally unrealistic). Even here in 1 Corinthians, Paul speaks of himself as an anomaly: different from the other apostles, different from the instructions Paul gives his own churches and different even from what Jesus said. That is the whole point. It is because Paul has the right to be paid and doesn't use it that his example is relevant to the Corinthian behaviour over idol food.

So why doesn't he? There are two reasons. The first is theological and relates to the nature of his call to preach in the first place: "I am compelled to preach. Woe to me if I do not preach the gospel!" (1 Corinthians **9:16**). Although modern preachers sometimes quote this of themselves and may experience echoes of what Paul experienced, we should remember that Paul's commission to preach the gospel to the Gentiles was genuinely unique: the risen Christ had appeared to him, in person, and told him what to do (Acts 9; 22; 26). The dramatic nature of Paul's conversion has profoundly shaped the way in which Christian preachers have described their own calls to ministry ever since (as you can see if you read the stories of people like Augustine, Luther and Wesley), but the essence of it was unrepeatable. Paul says this himself later (1 Corinthians 15:9), and sees the compulsion laid upon him at that moment as so strong that he would be under a curse ("woe to me") if he didn't obey. When people do things by choice, they get paid for them, and rightly so—but Paul is not doing it by choice in this sense, so he doesn't get paid (**9:17**). He is more like a slave than an employee. Instead of payment, Paul gets the reward of being able to "offer [the gospel] free of charge, and so not make use of my full rights as a preacher of the gospel" (**v 18**).

The image of the slave becomes explicit in the second reason, which is cross-cultural and contextual. Paul does not see himself merely as a slave of Christ but as a slave of those to whom he has been sent to preach. He is free, but he has become enslaved in order to win as many people as possible for Christ (**v 19**)—and slaves, by and large, are unpaid. So Paul is, too.

But Paul's "slavery" to all people does not just mean that he does not receive a salary. It means that he becomes like the people he is trying to reach, refusing to exercise his freedoms for the sake of winning them for the gospel. This, of course, is exactly what he is trying to get the Corinthians to do: to refuse to exercise their freedom to eat idol food for the sake of winning their brothers and sisters. And Paul does this wherever he goes and for whomever he is preaching to. If his audience is Jewish, he goes Jewish. If they are law-observant, he lives that way, even though he is free from the law (**v 20**). If they are Gentiles, and have no idea what the law is, he lives that way too (although clearly he continues to live under the "law of Christ", **v 21**). If they are "weak"—like those in the church that he mentioned in 8:10—then he becomes "weak", limiting his diet or whatever it is to win them as well. He has become, in one of the most famous lines in the whole letter, "all things to all people so that by all possible means I might save some" (**9:22**): so that he might receive not money but the blessings that come from the gospel (**v 23**). It makes you wonder whether the people who use that phrase—"The problem is, she's trying to be all things to all men"—know where it comes from, or that it was originally an argument for refusing to receive a salary or to eat in pagan temples.

Paul's Race

The last paragraph in the chapter is a hinge, joining together the two major arguments that Paul is making. In chapters 8 – 9, he has explained that the Corinthians should not eat idol food in pagan temples because it could destroy their weaker brothers and sisters, and he has used himself as an extended illustration of what it looks like to lay down your "rights" and "freedom" for the sake of others. In chapter 10, he will make the far more challenging argument that eating idol food in pagan temples is fundamentally idolatrous, and that if the Corinthian Christians continue doing it, they will face divine judgment. The first argument is based on love of neighbour; the second is based on love of God. And this little paragraph transitions us from one to the other.

Paul's apostolic ministry is motivated not by money but by a desire to gain a "reward" (**v 18**) and to "share in [the gospel's] blessings" (**v 23**). That requires self-discipline. It requires zeal and diligence and self-denial. If you practise those things, well and good. If you don't, you run the risk of losing out on the reward you are living for—something which Israel tragically discovered in the wilderness, as Paul will remind them in 10:1-13.

The Christian life, in that sense, is like a race. There is a "prize"—resurrection life with Christ for all eternity—but you have to pursue it and "run" in such a way as to get it (**9:24**). If you take athletics seriously (and the Corinthians hosted the Isthmian Games every two years, so they probably did), it involves a careful training regime, in which people make all sorts of sacrifices because they want to win. They avoid eating certain things. They exert themselves daily. They overcome their carnal desires. And the Corinthians did all that because they wanted a crown made of leaves! How much more should we Christians, who are pursuing a crown that will last for ever (**v 25**), exert ourselves and avoid eating certain things—idol food, perhaps?—in order to get it!

That is what Paul does, anyway. Given how secure Paul is in his walk with Jesus and how certain he is that the Lord will keep believers strong to the end (for example 1:7-9), you might think he would just amble through life, breezily confident that he will get the "prize" or the "crown" no matter what happens. Plenty of Christians have lived that way—including, by the looks of things, some of the Corinthians—but Paul doesn't. He doesn't "run aimlessly" like someone who doesn't know where the finish line is. He doesn't flail around like a shadow boxer, unaware that there is a real enemy to fight (**9:26**). No, he brings his body into submission, refusing to allow his carnal desires to dominate his life, so that he might not be "disqualified for the prize" (**v 27**). Considering how the Corinthians have been dominated by carnal desires for sex (chapters 5 – 7) and food (chapters 8 – 10), it is an enormously powerful illustration—and one which has a lot to say in a culture like ours, where "my freedom" and "my rights" have an almost untouchable status.

But it also raises a sticky question. If Paul has to run in such a way as to not be "disqualified for the prize", does that mean that Christians can fall short of their eternal hope through disobedience? Does Paul's attitude here serve as a warning to complacent disciples? As we enter chapter 10, we are about to find out.

Questions for reflection

1. What are your expectations about your standard of life? Is there any way in which laying down one of those expectations could help you to serve God better?

2. In what specific ways are you being called to "become all things to all people" for the sake of Christ?

3. Is there a particular area of life where you need to pursue greater self-discipline and self-denial in order to "run in such a way as to get the prize"?

7. THE TROUBLE WITH IDOLATRY

1 Corinthians is a letter full of warnings.

Build carefully in the church, or you'll see your labour go up in flames (3:10-15). If you destroy God's temple, God will destroy you (3:17). Hand the incestuous man over to Satan for the destruction of the flesh; if you don't, that little bit of mould will spread throughout the whole loaf (5:1-13). People who engage in sexual immorality or idolatry or theft or greed will not inherit the kingdom of God (6:9-10). Eating idol food in a pagan temple could destroy your brother or sister (8:7-13). Run in order to win the prize, so that you don't get disqualified from it (9:24-27). If you share the Lord's Supper in an unworthy manner, you will face judgment, and that's why some of you have got sick and even died (11:27-30). If anyone has no love for the Lord, let them be accursed (16:22). When we list them like that—and without mentioning the powerful assurances Paul gives alongside them—their frequency and intensity can seem overwhelming.

But by far the longest and most dramatic warning comes here in chapter 10. The presenting issue is still idol food, as it has been since 8:1, and the practice of eating it in the dining rooms or precincts of pagan temples. Here, however, the rationale for Paul's objection changes. It is not just because eating idol food is not loving to your neighbour, since it could destroy their faith (8:7-13), and so you should renounce your "rights" and "freedoms" for the sake of others (9:1-27). It is also because eating idol food in such a context is not loving to God himself because it is fundamentally idolatrous to "partake of the table of the Lord and the table of demons" (10:21). And in order to make this point as powerfully as possible, Paul turns to the most obvious—and scariest—example he can think of: a biblical story in which a huge group of saved people commit idolatry and thereby forfeit their inheritance: "For I do not want you to be ignorant of the fact, brothers and sisters, that our ancestors were all under the cloud and that they all passed through the sea" (**v 1**).

The reference is to the exodus generation. They all left Egypt with Moses, they were all guided by the pillar of cloud by day and the pillar of fire by night, and they all crossed the Red Sea. The word "all" is going to be important in this section; it's not that there were some people who had a genuine spiritual experience and therefore persevered, and others who didn't and therefore didn't. No: they all had the same blessings—the blessings of **redemption** by the blood of the lamb, God's presence in the cloud and an escape from their enemies through water. Implicitly, they were just like us.

Then Paul makes things more explicit. "They were all baptised into Moses in the cloud and in the sea" (**v 2**). Israel, like us, experienced a baptism: a journey through water which brought them to birth as a nation under the leadership of Moses, buried their past and drowned their enemies in the deep. (The power of the exodus story to explain what baptism does in a believer's life is remarkable, and I use it all the time as a pastor and a preacher.) And Israel were baptised not just "in the sea" but also "in the cloud". They were immersed in water and also in the glory-cloud of God's Spirit—again, like the Corinthian believers (as we will see when we get to 12:13).

There is more. "They all ate the same spiritual food and drank the same spiritual drink" (**10:3-4**). Our ancestors had an equivalent of baptism and they had an equivalent of the Lord's Supper: miraculous food and drink that God provided for them in the wilderness. They ate heavenly bread, in the form of manna. They drank heavenly liquid, in the form of water from the rock—and this rock, Paul explains, "was Christ" (**v 4**). This might sound like a bizarre point to make, until we remember that in the Song of Moses (the poem which effectively summarises the **Pentateuch**) Israel is repeatedly reminded that the "Rock" who has accompanied them on their desert travels, even to the point of feeding and watering them, is actually the Lord himself (Deuteronomy 32:4, 18, 30-31). So Israel, like the Corinthians, had a redemption story, an exodus journey, the experience of the Spirit in their midst and equivalents of both baptism and the Lord's Supper. They were just like us.

"Nevertheless, God was not pleased with most of them; their bodies were scattered in the desert" (1 Corinthians **10:5**). This is the twist in Paul's extended comparison, and it really sticks the knife in. *Israel had all the privileges that you have, he says: salvation, the Spirit and the sacraments. You might think that these blessings would somehow, almost magically, protect them (and even you) from the judgment of God. Yet God was not pleased with most of them. In fact, only two of those who were adults when they left Egypt got to enter the land God had promised them (Numbers 14:30). Mostly, their bodies ended up strewn across the desert.* Whoever has ears, let them hear.

Israel's Fall

The Corinthians may well have joined the dots already, but in case they haven't, Paul spells it out for them: "Now these things occurred as examples to keep us from setting our hearts on evil things as they did" (1 Corinthians **10:6**). The wilderness stories are not just stories: they are "examples"—*tupoi* (from which we get the word "**typology**"). The narrative tells us about Israel, but it also tells us about us. Primarily it serves as a warning, so that we see what happened to them and ensure that we do not copy their sin and experience the same fate.

The story of Israel in the wilderness is a brilliant example for Paul to have chosen. It is not just that Israel shared parallel blessings—**soteriological**, spiritual and **sacramental**—with the Corinthians. It is not even that they forfeited their inheritance (the promised land) and experienced divine judgment instead (death in the desert). It is that they forfeited their inheritance and faced divine judgment for idolatry and sexual immorality, the exact sins which the Corinthians are committing and which Paul is correcting in this letter.

The first calamity in Israel's wilderness journey, sometimes referred to as Israel's national "fall", revolved around idolatry (Exodus 32). The people asked **Aaron** to make them a golden calf, and ate and drank in its presence—you might even say that they ate "idol food" in front of it—and as a result 3,000 of them were killed by the sword and a great many others in a plague. Paul quotes directly from this passage and urges his readers to learn from their example: "Do not be idolaters, as some of them were; as it is written: 'The people sat down to eat and drink and got up to indulge in revelry'" (1 Corinthians **10:7**, quoting Exodus 32:6).

Israel's last rebellion, at the opposite end of their desert journey, was one of sexual immorality with **Moabite** women (Numbers 25). The immorality was so grotesque that at one point, as Moses was rebuking the people for their sin, an Israelite man took a **Midian-ite** woman into his tent in full view of the congregation; the pair ended up being skewered by the spear of **Phinehas** while having sex a few minutes later. The result of their sin, again, was a plague of divine judgment. The moral of the story is pretty obvious: "We should not commit sexual immorality, as some of them did—and in one day twenty-three thousand of them died" (1 Corinthians **10:8**).

The oddity here is that the book of Numbers records 24,000 people dying, not 23,000. It is possible that the Numbers figure is a deliberate "rounding up", with two thousand people dying per tribe, and that Paul is quoting a more exact figure (although where he got this figure from is unknown). It is possible that Paul is citing the number of people who died "in one day", and Numbers is talking about the total number who died (although again, nobody knows what source Paul might have been using). Other solutions have also been proposed, although the discrepancy remains something of a mystery. But in the grand scheme of things, whichever number we use, it is a massive act of judgment that should warn us all in the strongest terms: we must not commit sexual immorality and we must not participate in idol worship. Nor, while we are at it, must we "test Christ, as some of them did—and were killed by snakes" (**v 9**, referring to Numbers 21:5-6), or "grumble, as some of them did—and were killed by the destroying angel" (1 Corinthians **10:10**, based on Numbers 11:1; 14:2; 16:11). When people defy God, even if they are his chosen people, they are destroyed. "These things happened to them as examples and were written down as warnings for us, on whom the culmination of the ages has come" (1 Corinthians **10:11**).

It is worth noticing the connection between the two main sins in view here. Idolatry is frequently accompanied by sexual immorality in Scripture—the clearest example is probably that of **Solomon**, and the most graphic imagery is found in the books of Ezekiel and Hosea—and it is implied in the quotation Paul gives here, as the people get up to "play" (ESV) or "indulge in revelry" (**v 7**). Sexual immorality, likewise, is often accompanied by idolatry in the Old Testament; in the story Paul mentions (**v 8**), Israel is led astray to worship pagan gods and eat in their presence (Numbers 25:1-3). So Paul's "examples" are deliberately chosen to make his point. Israel, like the Corinthians, faced God's judgment over sexual immorality (Paul's focus in 1 Corinthians 5 – 7) and idolatrous food (chapters 8 – 10). In fact, the two sins reinforce each other. People who change their sexual partners will often end up changing their gods as well, and, if we are tempted to do either, then the scattering of Israelite bodies across the desert should be a warning to us all.

> People who change their sexual partners will often end up changing their gods as well.

Warnings and Assurances

Again, we are confronted with one of the great puzzles of reading this letter: how to fit together Paul's warnings (3:10-17; 5:1-13; 6:9-11; 8:7-13; 9:24-27; **10:1-22**; 11:27-30; 16:22) with his statements of reassurance (1:7-9; **10:13**; 15:20-28, 50-58). One minute Paul is guaranteeing the Corinthians that they will be blameless on the day of Christ and resurrected with him; the next he is warning them about the terrible divine judgment that will fall on them if they do not repent. It is genuinely difficult to see how the two fit together. Some readers emphasise the warnings and teach that genuine believers can forfeit their salvation; others emphasise the assurances and teach that they cannot. Paul emphasises both. There is a tension here.

Nowhere is that tension expressed more clearly than in **10:12-13**: "So, if you think you are standing firm, be careful that you don't fall!" (**v 12**). This warning is the whole point of the connection that Paul has been making in this chapter so far: be careful, don't fall, don't set your heart on evil as Israel did, or you will find yourself judged just as they were. And then in the very next verse we find a beautiful reassurance: "No temptation has overtaken you except what is common to mankind. And God is faithful; he will not let you be tempted beyond what you can bear. But when you are tempted, he will also provide a way out so that you can endure it" (**v 13**). It sounds as if Paul is saying that you need to be very careful not to fall into divine judgment, but that ultimately God will ensure that you don't.

I think that is exactly what he is saying, and not just here but throughout the letter. The warnings are real. If, as Christians, we "fall"—worship idols, continue in sexual immorality, destroy God's temple, or whatever it is—we will face God's judgment. And the assurances are real too. The faithfulness of God, which Paul appeals to in 1:9 as well as here, means that we will be preserved to the end, protected in the midst of temptation, and provided with a way of escape (**10:13**). I think Paul sees his warnings in this letter as one of the ways out of temptation that God has provided for the Corinthians, and for us. Paul believes that his warnings are a God-given means of ensuring that the Corinthians don't fall away and that they avoid the judgment that they would face if they did.

It sounds paradoxical, and in some ways it is, but it is not that different from how all serious warnings work. Here is how the great Victorian preacher Charles Spurgeon explained it:

"God preserves his children from falling away; but he keeps them by the use of means; and one of these is, the terrors of the law, showing them what would happen if they were to fall away. There is a deep precipice: what is the best way to keep any one from going down there? Why, to tell him that if he did he would inevitably be dashed to pieces."

("Final Perseverance," preached 20th April 1856, from New Park Street Pulpit, Volume 2)

It is very possible to warn someone that, if they approach a precipice (or participate in idol worship) they will be destroyed, while at the same time being confident that they will heed the warning and decide not to do it. Paul shows exactly that mixture of warning and confidence in the shipwreck story of Acts 27, for instance. He knows for certain that the crew will all be saved (Acts 27:22-25), but he warns them that if they don't follow his advice, they will drown (v 31). Both are true at once.

That, it seems to me, is exactly how Paul is reasoning here. And the reason for his confidence is not his own powers of persuasion or the shrillness of his warning but the character of the God who has called them: for "God is faithful" (1 Corinthians **10:13**).

Questions for reflection

1. Think of your own experience of blessings from God. How can these experiences help you to keep setting your heart on him?

2. Which of the "evil things" listed in verses 7-10 is the biggest temptation for you at the moment?

3. Which do you think you are in more need of hearing right now—warnings or assurance?

PART TWO

Idol Food in Pagan Temples

So far in chapter 10, Paul has developed his warning about idol food without actually referring to the practice directly. He has made allusions to it, in his choice of Old Testament examples which involve idol food as part of pagan worship (the golden calf and the Moabite apostasy). And we know that idol food has been the general topic of discussion since 8:1. But until now, he has not challenged any specific behaviour.

Finally he does: "Therefore, my dear friends, flee from idolatry" (**10:14**). This is the second time in the letter that Paul has told them to "flee" from something (the other was sexual immorality, in 6:18), and it is yet another instance of Paul making connections between what we worship and whom we sleep with. Some sins can be avoided or bypassed. But if you are tempted in areas of sexuality and idolatry then, like **Joseph** (Genesis 39:12), you need to run away as fast as you can. Idols, as the Corinthians themselves ought to know (1 Corinthians 12:2), have the power to ensnare people's hearts and shipwreck their lives. "I speak to sensible people; judge for yourselves what I say" (**10:15**).

Very few disciples, on hearing this, will argue that idolatry is actually acceptable. We all know that worshipping anyone other than God is completely incompatible with Christianity. What we do instead—and what the Corinthians had apparently done—is to argue that what we are doing is not really idolatrous; it's just a meal, just a fling, just a [insert equivalent here]. In the Corinthians' case, the logic was simple: idols don't really exist (8:4), so what harm can it possibly do to eat sacrificed food in a pagan temple?

It's a good question, and Paul's response comes in two parts. The first is to show the true character of eating and drinking in worship. Christians, of all people, ought to realise the spiritual power of eating and drinking in the context of worshipping God. The Lord's Supper, which Paul will address in much more detail in chapter 11, is not just food and drink; it is an act of worship which enacts our union with God and our union with one another. The cup for which we give thanks is a "participation"—the Greek word *koinonia* is often translated "fellowship" or "communion"—in the blood of Christ. The bread that we break is a "participation" in the body of Christ (**10:16**). When we share the bread and wine, we are not just eating and drinking; we are expressing fellowship, participation and communion with Christ and with one another. "We, who are many, are one body, for we all share the one loaf" (**v 17**).

The same principle held true in Jewish worship: "Consider the people of Israel: do not those who eat the sacrifices participate in the altar?" (**v 18**). To eat sacrificial food in a context of worship was to participate in the sacrifice—the act of worship—itself. If that is true in Christian worship (at the Lord's table), and if it was true in Jewish worship (at the temple altar), then it is true in pagan worship as well. The participants might think they're just having a meal, but they're actually worshipping an idol.

This takes us on to Paul's second response, which relates to the true character of idols. At a purely factual level, idols do not exist. Paul has already conceded this point (8:4) and does so again here: "Do I mean then that food sacrificed to an idol is anything, or that an idol is anything? No" (**10:19-20**). But demons exist. Principalities and powers exist. And when idols are worshipped by people who believe they are real and who serve them, demons exercise power over the worshipper. (We could say similar things about the belief in poltergeists or the ghosts of dead people today: they are not real, but they can exercise demonic power over people who believe they are.) So in one sense pagan sacrifices are offered to nobody at all, but in another sense they are offered to the darkest and most dangerous beings of all (**v 20**). Paul wants the Corinthians to have nothing to do with them.

Fundamentally, the table of demons and the table of the Lord are incompatible (**v 21**). You cannot have a sip from one cup and a sip from the other. As **Elijah** challenged the people of Israel on Mount Carmel, people cannot keep on wavering between two options: they have to choose between the Lord and an idol (1 Kings 18:21). For the Corinthians, that means making a decision to share the Lord's Supper and never to eat idol food in a pagan temple again. Dabbling in both risks provoking the Lord to jealousy, and if we do that, we will always come off worse (1 Corinthians **10:22**).

Sacrificial Food in the Meat Market

Paul has spent the best part of three chapters (8:1 – 10:22) explaining to the Corinthians why they should not eat idol food in the context of pagan worship. So it is somewhat unexpected, and potentially very confusing, when he appears to change tack. Idol food in Roman Corinth was not only something you would encounter in a pagan temple (which Paul prohibited); it was also something you would come across in the meat market (which Paul allows), or in a private home (which Paul will address in a moment). So although the discussion of idol food in pagan temples is finished, there are still a couple of loose ends for Paul to tie up. Ever mindful of the danger of **legalism** and the importance of Christian freedom, Paul wants to clarify that the problem with "idol food" is the "idol" rather than the "food"—the context rather than the content. Hence this brief section.

It comes in two short paragraphs. The essence of the first (**v 23-24**) is familiar to us by now, since we encountered it briefly in 1 Corinthians 6 and at length in chapters 8 – 9. It reflects the different visions of Christian freedom that characterise the Corinthians, for whom it is about rights ("I have the right to do anything"), and Paul, for whom it is about love ("No one should seek their own good, but the good of others"). Although it does not seem especially relevant to the question of buying sacrificial food in the meat market, it will be crucial for the way Paul handles the question of eating it in a private home. It also presents us with a wonderful summary of Christian ethics. As followers of Jesus, we are not just to ask whether something is lawful but whether it is loving. Plenty of things are not banned, but they are not beneficial either.

We are not just
to ask whether
something
is lawful but
whether it
is loving.

In the second paragraph, Paul gives his answer to the question of what believers should do when they go to the meat market. In a city like Corinth, the chances were that a sizeable proportion of the meat available in the city—perhaps even a large majority—had previously been offered as sacrifices to a pagan deity. So for a Corinthian Christian to avoid eating sacrificed food would involve either avoiding meat altogether or a pedantic (and probably unrealistic) enquiry into the origins of every meal they ate. Meat in Roman Corinth did not come shrink-wrapped in plastic, and the packaging did not stipulate whether the animals in question had been free-range, corn-fed or happy at the time of their deaths.

Paul's answer is sweeping, simple and liberating: "Eat anything sold in the meat market without raising questions of conscience" (**10:25**). This makes it crystal clear that Paul's problem with "idol food" in **verses 1-22** was not the meat but the meaning: Christians should not participate in pagan worship, but that doesn't mean that any meat which has previously been offered in sacrifice is permanently off limits. Quite the opposite, in fact, "for 'the earth is the Lord's, and everything in it'" (**v 26**, quoting Psalm 24:1). In Paul's world, as in ours, there were all sorts of people banning all sorts of foods for all sorts of reasons. Paul will have none of it, and regularly takes the opportunity to give asceticism a punch on the nose (Romans 14:4; Colossians 2:16; 1 Timothy 4:1-5), even as he insists that we should never do anything which causes our brothers or sisters to stumble. Christians are free to eat anything, and free not to. God created it; I can eat it; that settles it.

Sacrificial Food in Private Homes

The final scenario Paul considers is the one with the most complex answer. For all the elaborate length of Paul's discussion of idol food, his line on whether or not you can eat it is very simple: no. His take on buying from the meat market is at the opposite end of the scale when it comes to length, but again it is simple: yes. Private homes are a bit more complicated, though. There are a number of moving parts—you, your host, and any other guests who might be there—and that all needs to be factored in.

So Paul lays out the scenario. An unbeliever invites you to their home for a meal, and you want to go. In that situation, you should eat whatever they serve you, whether it includes meat or not, and you shouldn't raise any conscience questions about it (1 Corinthians **10:27**). This is the natural extension of the meat-market situation. There is meat in front of you; you don't know whether it was offered in sacrifice or not, but the earth is the Lord's and everything in it, so there's no point in worrying about it and needlessly offending your host. Enjoy your steak.

Then the scenario changes: now there is another guest there who tells you that the meat has been offered in sacrifice. (It is significant that the word used here, *hierothuton*, is different from the word *eidolothuton*. Paul seems to be differentiating between "sacrificial food", which is served as part of an ordinary meal in a home, and "idol food", which is served as part of pagan worship in a temple). That changes things. If the person who tells you is a believer, it suggests that they are concerned, and that your eating it could give them a problem along the lines that Paul has already discussed in chapter 8. Even if they are not a believer, it could still make things difficult for them, in that if they see a Christian knowingly eating sacrificial food, they might conclude that pagan sacrifice is compatible with Christianity. Different circumstances mean a different decision: "Do not eat it, both for the sake of the one who told you and for the sake of conscience" (**10:28**).

Again, however, Paul is clear that this is because of their conscience(s), not because of yours (**v 29**): "If I take part in the meal with thankfulness, why am I denounced because of something I thank God for?" (**v 30**). Even in his counsel to exercise caution and discernment, Paul is continually careful to ensure that his guidance not be twisted and turned into a prohibition, so he stresses that as long as the Corinthian Christian is receiving something with thankfulness, there is nothing to worry about. As he puts it in 1 Timothy 4:4, "Everything created by God is good, and nothing should be rejected if it is received with thanksgiving, because it is consecrated by the word of God and prayer".

God's Glory in Your Life

Paul's long and thoughtful section on food comes to a head in one of his most quotable sentences: "So whether you eat or drink or whatever you do, do it all for the glory of God" (1 Corinthians **10:31**). This is a super summary of Paul's teaching on everything, not just food. The glory of God is paramount. If you are taking part in something which God has given, do it with thankfulness for his grace and bounty. If you are abstaining from it, do it out of the desire that other people are not made to stumble, whether Jews, Greeks or other Christians (**v 32**). If you're cooking for a Muslim, go to the halal store. If you're in a culture where alcohol is frowned upon, go teetotal. If your friend becomes a vegan, learn some new recipes. If your neighbour invites you for a barbecue, eat what is set before you and thank God for making cows out of beef. Food and drink matter, but the glory of God matters more.

Paul himself, as we have seen in previous chapters, has walked the walk here. This is his whole philosophy of ministry: the glory of God comes before his own preferences for reputation and comfort (chapter 4), marrying and having children (chapter 7), earning and working (chapter 9), and eating and drinking. He is happy for people to be put off by the gospel (chapter 1), but he is not happy for them

to be put off by his conduct (chapter 9), so in every way he seeks "not
… my own good but the good of many, so that they may be saved"
(**10:33**). It could sound self-important, but Paul knows that Christians
do not just follow advice; we follow people. So his counsel to the Corinthians—and, in fact, the counsel of any pastor who is consistently
living out what they are teaching—is very straightforward: "Follow my
example, as I follow the example of Christ" (**11:1**).

Questions for reflection

1. How do verses 16-17 need to sharpen or shape your thinking
   about sharing the Lord's Supper?

2. When are you tempted to say, "It's just…" (see page 109)?

3. What different views about food do you encounter in your culture
   and among your neighbours? What will it look like for you to eat
   and drink for the glory of God?

8. COVERED HEADS AND BROKEN BREAD

There are five main blocks of material in 1 Corinthians, and now we enter the fourth one. We have seen Paul address leadership and division (chapters 1 – 4), sex and litigation (5 – 7) and idol food (8 – 10), and in the next few chapters the subject will be corporate worship (11 – 14). Considering the various problems he is going to address, it might surprise us that Paul starts by praising the Corinthians "for remembering me in everything and for holding to the traditions just as I passed them on to you" (**11:2**). Is he being ironic? Ingratiating? Personally I think it more likely that he is being truthful: they have asked him a genuine question, and he is pleased about that and happy to respond. But this sentence also enables him to underline the importance of "remembering" and "traditions", concepts which will prove significant later (v 23-26; see also 15:1-3).

A Question of the Head

The presenting issue in the first half of this chapter is head coverings, and what is appropriate for men and women in the context of Christian worship. It is a fiendishly difficult passage. Scholars continue to debate all kinds of issues that arise here, and five in particular are worth mentioning. One: We cannot be certain whether Paul is referring to wearing a covering over one's head, like a hood or a veil, or whether he is talking about the way people wear their hair. Two: We cannot be certain why he is concerned about it. Three: Much of Paul's argument is built on a wordplay around the word "head" (*kephale*), but there is disagreement about what this metaphor actually means. Four: The section contains a couple of theological curveballs that would be challenging in any passage, like "the head of Christ is God" (**11:3**), or "woman is the glory of man" (**v 7**), or "because of the angels" (**v 10**). Five: The relations and differences between men and women are enormously controversial in our generation, and therefore any passage that addresses the subject so directly is bound to divide opinion. (There are two passages about men and women in this letter, and in both cases there are serious **evangelical** scholars who argue that some or all of them do not come from Paul—see, for example, Gordon Fee, *The First Epistle to the Corinthians,* pages 699-708, on 14:33-35; and Lucy Peppiatt, *Women and Worship at Corinth,* on **11:2-16**.) And all that is without mentioning a sixth issue, which is probably the most pressing for Christian readers: whatever Paul is saying, what on earth do we do about it?

With all those questions swirling around, it is easy to get lost. So let me put my cards on the table. I think Paul is saying that men should not wear a hood, veil or cloak over their heads when praying or prophesying, and that women should. I think he teaches this in order to acknowledge and represent the distinctions between women and men in corporate worship. I think he gives three main theological reasons for this, based on honour and shame (**v 3-6**), the relationship between men and women (**v 7-12**), and the nature of things (**v 13-16**). And I think that when it comes to application, we need to remember that sexual differences are represented in different cultures in different ways, and therefore that we may need to "translate" the symbols (in this case, head coverings) into our culture, in order to preserve their meaning.

Honour and Shame

The most difficult biblical concepts are the ones that look the easiest. If you come across something very unfamiliar in Scripture—putting your hand under someone's thigh, for instance, or swapping sandals (Genesis 24; Ruth 4)—you immediately know you don't understand it, so you investigate to find out what it meant in the ancient world, and what a modern equivalent might be (say, signing a contract). But if you are already familiar with a concept, you don't bother; you assume it meant the same thing then as it means now. It's a common problem, and nowhere is it more of an issue than with Paul's use of the "head" metaphor here: "The head of every man is Christ, and the head of the woman is man, and the head of Christ is God" (1 Corinthians **11:3**).

To most of us, the "head" is simply the one in charge. The head of a school, or a department, or the armed forces is the boss. Heads have authority to tell other people what to do and to expect obedience from them, and they are almost always paid more and esteemed more. So when we see Paul saying that the "head" of the woman is man—or that the "head" of Christ is God—we read it through the lens of command and authority, whether or not that is what Paul meant.

> The "head" is not about command and control, like in a Western organisation, but about honour and shame, like in an eastern family.

Here, as it happens, that reading is partially right. The relationships between husbands and wives in Corinth, and between God and Jesus during his incarnation, did indeed involve some measure of authority, as most scholars agree. But the heart of Paul's picture is not command and control, like in a Western organisation. It is honour and shame, like in an Eastern family. The "head" is not primarily the one in charge, or even the origin or source of everything else (although he is usually both); the "head" is the prominent, uppermost, supreme or pre-eminent one, the one whose reputation is either honoured or shamed by the actions of others. Word studies are often very useful, but if we want to understand Paul's **metaphor** and the way it relates to what people wear on their heads, there is no substitute for spending a few days in a Middle Eastern village.

Once you see it, you notice the language everywhere. If a man prays or prophesies while wearing a veil or a hood, he "dishonours his head" (**v 4**), namely Christ. If a woman prays or prophesies without wearing a veil or a hood, she "dishonours her head" (**v 5**), namely her husband. In much of the world, even today, a man would look disgraceful if he wore a particular type of clothing or haircut, and a woman would look disrespectful or downright sexually promiscuous if she refused to wear the hijab, let her hair down, and exposed her neck and shoulders. Dressing like this would not just bring shame on her but on her husband as well. She might as well go the whole way and cut off all her hair, like a temple prostitute—and since that is obviously a disgrace, it follows that she should keep her head covered (**v 6**).

Men and Women

This could all sound rather arbitrary, but it isn't. It actually reflects the creation of man and woman right at the beginning: "A man ought not to cover his head, since he is the image and glory of God; but woman is the glory of man" (**v 7**). The differences between men and women, which Paul is arguing need to be reflected in their appearances, are not merely the result of cultural customs; they stem from the fact that God created man first and then created woman "from" him (**v 8**) and "for" him (**v 9**). So if men pray or prophesy while looking like women, or women pray or prophesy while looking like men (or even prostitutes, as we have just seen), the distinctiveness of the sexes is undermined, in the very context—public speech to and on behalf of God—where it should be most clearly upheld.

Notice what Paul does not say. He does not say that men bear the image of God and women do not, or that men are superior and women are inferior. (His comment that men are the glory of God while women are the glory of man has sometimes been taken that way, but it does not imply this at all. I have an apple tree in my garden, which produces apples, from which we make apple crumble. The crumble is the glory of the apple—it reflects its goodness in every way, and brings honour to it—and the apple is the glory of the tree—and none of the three are superior or inferior to the other two.) Men and women bear God's image together, and reflect God's glory on earth in different and complementary ways.

As if to ensure that he is not misunderstood on this point, Paul adds two further considerations. First, the woman "ought to have authority over her own head" (**v 10**), which she should express by wearing a covering. The alternative is to expose her head to indignity by unveiling it, and that would be shameful not only at a human level but also "because of the angels", who join in worshipping God when the church gathers together. Second, men and women are interdependent in the Lord (**v 11**). The sexes need one another to flourish, and in fact to exist in the first place. Woman came from man in the beginning, but ever since then men have come from women, even as both ultimately come from God (**v 12**).

So whatever else we may say about this passage, it is not an argument for the suppression of women. Lest we forget, Paul is regulating what women should wear while praying and prophesying in the gathered church; he is talking about women delivering Spirit-inspired revelation to the people of God, like Hannah and Huldah and Mary (1 Samuel 2:1-10; 2 Kings 22:14-20; Luke 1:46-56). So yes, Paul believes that men and women are beautifully different and should reflect that difference in physical ways in the congregation. But he also believes that we need one another to exist, to flourish, and to fully reflect the glory of God. May our churches express both truths together.

The Nature of Things

Paul's third and final argument for the practice he is commending here—that women should wear head coverings when praying or prophesying, and men should not—is probably the easiest to understand, and it is based on what he calls "the very nature of things" (1 Corinthians **11:14**). Men in Roman Corinth did not normally have long hair, and if they did, it would be seen as shameful; in the only Corinthian statues we have showing men with long hair, the men are captives and are clearly being represented as weak, effeminate softies. Women, by contrast, did wear their hair long, and it was regarded as beautiful and glorious (**v 15**), as in many cultures it still is. Well, if the Corinthians accept that it is "proper" for a woman to have long hair, and "a disgrace" for a man—which Paul knows they do (**v 13-14**)—then they must surely concede that men should not have their heads "covered", and women should. It is staringly obvious even by their own standards.

All this raises the crucial question of how we apply Paul's teaching here today. Some churches follow Paul's instructions to the letter: women cover their heads when praying or prophesying and men don't. Others ignore it altogether, dismissing it as "cultural". The latter is more common but in many ways more problematic; the Bible cannot be neatly divided up into "timeless" bits, which we still need to live by now, and "cultural" bits, which thankfully we don't—and even if it could be, Paul's arguments here are drawn from Genesis and the Trinity, among others, which look ominously timeless. But I think the former is misguided as well, because the process of what I call "symbolic translation" has not been considered. Physical symbols mean different things in contemporary London and ancient Corinth, and if we don't "translate" the symbols from one culture to another, we risk all sorts of misunderstandings.

In Bulgaria, for instance, nodding your head means "no" and shaking your head means "yes". So if you are travelling there and you want to indicate a yes, you need to change your gesture in order to preserve your meaning, or you will quickly cause a lot of frustration. We do this all the time as we read Scripture: when we read the exhortation to "greet one another with a holy kiss" (Romans 16:16; 1 Corinthians 16:20; 2 Corinthians 13:12; 1 Thessalonians 5:26; 1 Peter 5:14), we don't dismiss it as "merely cultural", but nor do we ask our welcome team to start kissing everybody. Instead, we take the meaning of the physical symbol—an expression of familial love and affection that brothers and sisters would use—and then we translate it into symbols that exist within our own culture for familial love and affection (a hug, a kiss, a handshake, a fist bump, or whatever it is).

We need to go through the same process with 1 Corinthians 11. Paul's teaching on head coverings is intended to preserve appropriate distinctions between the sexes, so that men look like men and women look like women, and to avoid a sexually provocative or maritally inappropriate appearance in gathered worship. So how do we communicate those things in our culture? In some parts of the world, the answer would look very similar to that in Roman Corinth: women would cover their heads and men would not. In much of the West today, it might look quite different. Men might have long hair, but they would not prophesy in mascara and lipstick. Women need not look as if they have walked out of *Pride and Prejudice*, but they shouldn't look as if they have walked off the set of *Love Island* either. You get the idea.

Paul wants the glory of maleness and femaleness to be represented in the gathered church, and especially in public speech. It brings glory to God, honour to both men and women, clarity to angels, and unity to the church. If anyone wants to be argumentative about it, then they should know that all Paul's congregations do the same (**v 16**).

Questions for reflection

1. How can you make sure you honour God when you are gathered with your church?

2. What is the equivalent of head coverings and hair length in your setting? What practical implications are there in this for you?

3. In general in your relationships with the opposite sex, how can you reflect the fact that men and women are different but not independent?

PART TWO

Communion Chaos

I have been in some fairly disastrous Christian meetings in my time, and I doubt I'm the only one. I have been part of chaotic scenes where visitors are terrified and nobody knows what is going on, least of all the pastor. I have sung songs where the worship leader is playing the verse but singing the chorus. I have seen people step up to offer a brief testimony, and twenty minutes later they are still talking (and nobody is listening). I have heard sermons so unbiblical they make you want to shout at the preacher, and invitations offered that sound like the work of snake-oil salesmen. But I have never thought, let alone said, what Paul says about Communion at Corinth: "I have no praise for you, for your meetings do more harm than good" (**v 17**).

Over the course of the next four chapters, we will come across a number of things that need correcting in the Corinthians' corporate worship. So it is notable that the only one which brings this level of rebuke—*Seriously, you lot would have done more good if you had stayed at home and not met together at all*—is their practice of the Lord's Supper. Partly that reflects the severity of the errors involved, as we will see. But partly it shows how serious breaking bread is, and how much damage we can do to each other by abusing it, as compared with anything else in our worship service. This is the body and blood of Jesus. We are treading on holy ground.

The fundamental problem in Corinth, as we have seen many times already, is division (**v 18**). Paul has heard reports of this, perhaps from Chloe's people again, and he is predisposed to believe it; he adds, clearly sarcastically (given his opposition to division throughout the letter), that "no doubt there have to be differences among you to show which of you have God's approval" (**v 19**). They are divided over leadership, and sexual ethics, and litigation, and idol food, so it is no great surprise that they are divided at the Lord's Table as well. But in this case, division completely changes the nature of what they are doing. It is not that they are celebrating the Lord's Supper deficiently; it is that by making the centre of Christian unity a source of division, they are not really eating the Lord's Supper at all (**v 20**). They have taken the ultimate act of self-giving and made it an act of self-serving. They have turned the cross of Christ into a bunfight.

> The Lord's Supper is supposed to be a communal meal, with everyone united around the same table.

It is supposed to be a communal meal, with everyone united around the same table and with everyone demonstrating the same need for grace. In social terms, it is meant to feel like a potluck dinner, with everyone sharing together no matter how much or little they can afford. But instead it has become an aeroplane meal: everyone has their own private supper, with the rich eating First Class and even getting drunk in the process, and the poor getting leftovers (if that) in the seat at the back by the toilets (**v 21**). *What on earth is the point of that? If all you want is a meal,* Paul says, *you can eat at home. Yet you insist on doing it during the most sacred moment we have, despising the church of God and "humiliating those who have nothing" (v 22)*. He is dumbfounded.

Three practical points are also worth noting here. The first is that the Eucharist is shared "when you come together as a church" (**v 18**), a point that Paul makes five times in this section (**v 17, 18, 20, 33, 34**). It is a corporate act for the church when they gather, not a private and individual one which is intended to take place in isolation from other believers. The second point is that we are clearly dealing with wine rather than non-alcoholic grape juice here, since it is possible to get drunk from it (**v 21**); we can debate whether or not we should use wine ourselves, but it seems clear that the Corinthians certainly did. And the third point is that Paul, as I will show in this chapter, uses a number of different words for this meal. He has already referred to "Communion" (10:16-17, NKJV), and "the Lord's table" (10:21); here he gives us our word "Eucharist" (**11:24**; *eucha-risteo* means "give thanks"), and talks about "the Lord's Supper" (**v 20**) and breaking bread (**v 24**). Each term communicates some-thing slightly different about the beauty and significance of this meal. So although different **denominations** tend to stick with one or two names for it—house churches break bread, **high churches** celebrate the Eucharist, and so on—we might be better served by using all of them. Paul does.

The Meaning of the Lord's Supper

11:23-26 is probably the most well-known paragraph in the letter outside of chapter 13. It forms the centre of the Communion **liturgy** in many churches (including those which don't generally like the idea of liturgy!), and you can see why. It is dense, rich, memorable prose. Paul has managed to condense the essence of the **sacrament** and the power of the death of Christ into less than one hundred words.

His opening sentence contains a powerful wordplay that is diffi-cult to capture in English. We might get close if we put it like this: "For I received from the Lord what I also *handed over (paradidomi)* to you: the Lord Jesus, on the night he was *handed over (paradidomi)*, took bread" (**11:23**). Mostly we translate the second of these as "be-trayed", so we miss the connection. But Paul is quite deliberately as-sociating his "handing over" of the practice and wording of the Lord's Supper with the "handing over" of Jesus on the night before he died. This raises an interesting possibility. It suggests that Paul is not simply referring to the betrayal of Jesus by Judas but to the handing over of Jesus by a whole range of people in the Gospel story: Judas, Peter, the soldiers, the chief priests, the council, Pilate, Herod, the crowd and ultimately God himself, who "handed over" Jesus to death for our transgressions (Acts 2:23; Isaiah 53:12). *Jesus was handed over to death for our salvation,* Paul is saying, *and when I came to Corinth, I handed over the meaning of that death and the meal by which we remember it.*

This marvellous summary paragraph shows us what we actually do as we celebrate the Lord's Supper. As we have already seen, we look up in gratitude to God, beginning with a prayer of thanksgiving (*eucharisteo*) to God for his gifts to us in the bread and wine, representing the body and blood. We look back, in remembrance of Jesus, whose body was broken "for you" (1 Corinthians **11:24**) and whose blood inaugurates "the new covenant in [his] blood" (**v 25**). We look forward, prophetically proclaiming the day when the Lord will return and we will share new bread and new wine in the Father's kingdom (**v 26**). And as we will see in the next section, we also look within (**v 28**) and look around at the rest of the body (**v 29**), with whom we are one despite being many (10:17).

What Paul does not do, here or anywhere else, is elaborate on what the words "this is my body" (**11:24**) actually mean, and in what way the bread and the wine "are" the body and blood of Christ. Are the bread and wine essentially transformed into the body and blood, even as they continue to look like bread and wine (the Roman Catholic view)? Are they physically both bread and wine and the body and blood, at the same time (the **Lutheran** view)? Are they just symbols which memorialise the body and blood, helping us to remember the cross but without bringing the presence of Christ in any unique way (the **Zwinglian** view)? Or do they effect Christ's spiritual presence as we eat and drink, but without making him physically present (the Reformed, or **Calvinistic**, view)?

We all have our convictions on these matters, and it is right that we do. But we should always be challenged by the fact that these precious words come to us in the context of warnings against dividing, despising and dismissing the church (**v 17-22**). And we should always be encouraged by the fact that Paul ends this paragraph by reminding us of the return of Christ (**v 26**), when all the redeemed, whatever our sacramental theologies, will drink the vintage of the kingdom served by Jesus himself (see Matthew 26:29).

Be Warned

The third section of this chapter is the natural result of the first two. If this meal is as meaningful and powerful as Jesus has said it is (1 Corinthians **11:23-26**), and if the Corinthians are bungling it as comprehensively as Paul has heard they are (**v 17-22**), then we would expect a call for repentance and a warning of judgment. That is exactly what we get.

When we come to the table, we are sharing in the body and blood of Jesus. This is not a snack or a social event. It is not something to be flippant about. So if we do this "in an unworthy manner"—whether in the specific way that the Corinthians are doing that, by not "discerning the body of Christ" (**v 29**), or in any other form of unrepentant sin—we will be "guilty of sinning against the body and blood of the Lord" (**v 27**). That sounds serious, and indeed it is. So before coming to the table, "everyone ought to examine themselves" (**v 28**).

This is not a call for moral perfection. The Eucharist is not a congratulatory banquet for the sinless; it is a sustaining meal for repentant sinners, who are hungry and thirsty for righteousness but know they have fallen short. So this call for self-examination is not aimed at excluding those who have sinned (or none of us would dare approach the table!) It is aimed at excluding those who do not care whether or not they have sinned: the unrepentant, the proud, "those who eat and drink without discerning the body of Christ" (**v 29**). Nowhere has this been more clearly expressed than in the Heidelberg Catechism and Question 81: "Who should come to the Lord's table?" Answer: "Those who are displeased with themselves because of their sins, but who nevertheless trust that their sins are pardoned and that their remaining weakness is covered by the suffering and death of Christ." Communion is for repentant believers.

Those who are not repentant or not believers should stay away from the Lord's Supper, lest they "eat and drink judgment on themselves" (**v 29**). If that was all Paul had said, we would probably assume that he was talking about final judgment. But to our surprise, he immediately clarifies that this is not what he is talking about; he is actually referring to experiences of divine judgment in the present. *As a result of your abusive practices at the table,* he explains, *some of you have become weak or sick (v 30). Others have died! If only you had been a bit more discerning about yourselves, this would all have been avoided (v 31).*

Modern readers often find that astonishing, even shocking. Is Paul really saying that God might make a person physically unwell, or even kill them, as an act of judgment for dishonouring the Lord? Indeed he is. The book of Acts contains at least four examples of exactly that (Acts 5:4-5, 9-10; 12:23; 13:9-11), one of which was enacted by Paul himself, and he is fairly clear about it here. Sin leads to judgment.

But notice why. The purpose of this present judgment, Paul says, is to save people from eternal judgment (something we have come across before in this letter with the incestuous man in 1 Corinthians 5:4-5). The key sentence comes in **11:32**: when we are judged (*krino*), we are being disciplined (*paideuo*) so that we are not condemned (*katakrino*). Yes, God brings judgment on his people sometimes. Yes, it may result in sickness or even death. But this judgment should be understood as discipline—as correction, as training—in order that we do not face condemnation. That distinction is critical in the exercise of church discipline: temporal judgment ("discipline") can save people from eternal judgment ("condemnation"). It is also pretty central in parenting.

Having called for repentance and warned of judgment, Paul concludes by summarising his instructions: *You should all eat together, rather than some wolfing everything down and leaving others without, and that way you will avoid the judgment I have been talking about (v 33-34). My other instructions can wait for now.*

Questions for reflection

1. As you celebrate the Lord's Supper, do you most often find yourself looking up in gratitude, back in remembrance, forward in proclamation of Jesus' return, within at your own sin, or around at the rest of the church? Do you ever miss any of these out?

2. Do you think you take Communion seriously enough?

3. In your church, what could you do to ensure that Communion is a genuine sign of unity for all believers?

9. GIFTS, LORDSHIP AND LOVE

After spending half a chapter on head coverings and half a chapter on the Lord's Supper, Paul now launches into a three-chapter discussion of spiritual gifts. The sheer length of this section tells us something. Admittedly, we have to be careful about determining Paul's priorities on the basis of how much time he spends on a topic, or the Corinthians would have had to conclude that head coverings were as important as the cross. But the fact that Paul gives so much attention to the specifics of how life in the Spirit works in a corporate context—especially when he has dispensed with incest, lawsuits, prostitution and divorce so quickly—surely indicates its importance to him.

We are already familiar with the little phrase "Now about…" (**12:1**), which signals that Paul is responding to a question from the Corinthians' letter (see 7:1, 25; 8:1; 16:1, 12). The question in this case is about spiritual gifts—*pneumatika* could mean "spiritual things" or even "spiritual people", but Paul's focus is mainly on the gifts here—a subject about which Paul does not want them to be "uninformed". With spiritual gifts, as so often in the Christian life, a little knowledge is a dangerous thing. The Corinthians "know" that when they were pagans they were "influenced and led astray to dumb [or mute] idols" (**12:2**). That is a good start. But Paul wants to make known something else, which is foundational to understanding and using spiritual gifts appropriately. The acid test of whether the Holy Spirit is at work is the declaration of the lordship of Jesus (**v 3**).

That might or might not be the first test we would think of. It certainly doesn't seem to be what the Corinthians thought. They were more impressed by miraculous power, prophetic insight, faith that can move mountains and the languages of men and angels—and so are many of us today. For Paul, however, the Spirit's activity is shown in a much more foundational way. If a person curses Jesus, they are not speaking by the Spirit (even if they appear to have great power). If a person declares, "Jesus is Lord", they are speaking by the Spirit (even if they don't appear to have great power). In a world where people appraise spirituality in all kinds of ways, the simplicity of this test—is Jesus being exalted as Lord?—is both freeing and encouraging.

There is a trinitarian logic to it as well. Look at the flow of **verse 3**: "No one who is speaking by the *Spirit* of *God* says, '*Jesus* be cursed,' and no one can say, '*Jesus* is *Lord,*' except by the *Holy Spirit*" (emphasis mine). All three members of the Trinity are involved when a person declares that Jesus is Lord. That is what the Spirit desires more than anything, and that is why the Father sent him. So as wonderful as spiritual gifts are—and Paul is passionately committed to them, as these chapters will show—the most powerful thing the Spirit can do in a person is to bring them to acknowledge the kingship of Christ. We must not try to be more spiritual than God.

Father, Son and Spirit are all active in the giving of spiritual gifts, too (**v 4-6**). Paul frequently teaches in explicitly trinitarian ways, and this is one of the best examples. There are different kinds of gifts, but one Spirit; different kinds of service, but one Lord; different kinds of working, but one God. This reinforces the idea that the Trinity collaborate together, and therefore that the activity of the Spirit must not be divorced from the work of the Father and the Son. But it also introduces the idea which will dominate the rest of chapter 12: unity in diversity. Yes, there are a great many spiritual gifts—which Paul also talks about as kinds of "service" and "working"—but there is one Spirit, one Lord, one God. In the world, diversity feels as if it is pulling against unity: either you remain united and squash your differences or you express your differences and fragment into a thousand pieces. In the church, it is different. Diversity serves unity, and unity celebrates diversity. The people of God are many, yet we are one body (10:17).

The gifts of God are many, yet they have one Giver and one purpose (**12:4-6**). The Persons of God are many—Father, Son and Spirit—yet there is one God.

Spiritual Gifts and the Good of the Church

The exaltation of Jesus as Lord is the clearest sign of the Spirit's work. But another clear indication is what Paul calls "the common good" (**v 7**). Spiritual gifts are given for the advantage of everybody in the church—a point Paul will make frequently in these chapters. They are not given so that the individual using them can parade their spirituality, or show off, or have an **ecstatic experience** which brings no benefit to anyone else. Nor are they given to a small set of elite believers to mark them out as genuinely spiritual in contrast to the rest of the church. The manifestation of the Spirit is given "to each one"—including you—for the benefit of everybody. (Although the word "manifestation" is sometimes associated with weird phenomena in the contemporary church, the word *phanerosis* simply refers to the Spirit's power being disclosed, exhibited and put on display.)

To show what this looks like in a congregation, Paul gives a number of examples (**v 8-10**). It is important to stress that these are examples, rather than a comprehensive list of every gift the Spirit might give. I remember hearing the story of someone who had previously been a member of the People's Temple, the cult led by Jim Jones many of whose adherents died in a mass murder/suicide in Guyana in 1978. This person was asked why they had left, and they said it was because the group advertised an event where people could "come and hear the man who possesses all nine spiritual gifts". If anyone ever talks like that, run. These nine are examples of spiritual gifts, not a complete catalogue—there is no mention of apostles, teachers, helping or guidance, all of which appear later in the chapter (**v 27-31**)—and Paul's whole point here is that everyone has something and nobody has everything.

The "message of wisdom" and the "message of knowledge" (**v 8**) are the hardest to define because they could refer to a whole range of things. Paul might mean preaching the gospel, given the way he talks about proclaiming the "message" of God's "wisdom" in chapter 2. In charismatic circles the "word of knowledge" has become a technical term for a supernatural insight into a specific person's circumstances, often followed by a healing; there is nothing especially harmful about this, but there is no evidence for it here, and I think Paul would probably just describe that as prophecy. Paul might simply be referring here to the God-given ability to read a situation and speak wisely and knowledgeably into it, which is my own view.

The Corinthians, as we know, are proud of their "wisdom" and "knowledge", and throughout this letter Paul has corrected their misunderstandings of both, while pointing to the Spirit as their true source.

Some have "faith by the same Spirit" (**12:9**). Although all faith is ultimately a result of the Spirit's work, Paul is not talking about saving faith here; that is common to all believers rather than given to some in particular. More likely, he means the gift that some people have of being able to believe God for apparently impossible things, whether physical healing, miraculous provision, missionary breakthrough or whatever it is. Others have "gifts of healing by that one Spirit". Although all believers can and should pray for healing, and elders in particular are called to do so (James 5:14-16), healings are gifts from God—not, we should note, rewards for sufficient levels of godliness, certainty or technique—which some have far more than others.

Some have the gift of working miracles (1 Corinthians **12:10**), as Paul himself clearly did. Some are able to prophesy or speak in languages or interpret languages spoken by others (and we will see what these gifts are and how to use them when we reach chapter 14). Some have the gift of "distinguishing between spirits" (**12:10**): the spiritual discernment to tell whether something is genuinely the work of the Holy Spirit or whether it is demonic, or coming from the spirit of the world (what we might call the zeitgeist), or something else. All of these gifts, and more besides, "are the work of one and the same Spirit, and he distributes them to each one, just as he determines" (**v 11**).

For many Western readers, this raises an inevitable question: do these gifts continue? Should we expect miracles, healings, prophecy and languages in the church today? We will come back to this question as we work through these chapters, but it is a good rule of thumb to assume that New Testament passages apply to us unless it is clear from the context that they don't. Given that Paul is not talking about a unique subset of the church but rather the entire congregation ("all of them", "everyone", "each one", and so on), we are best off assuming that he is talking about all Christians, at least for now, and listening carefully to see what we can learn.

Spiritual Gifts and the Unity of the Body

One of the tragic ironies of this letter and the way it has been interpreted is that spiritual gifts are given to build unity but have somehow become a source of division. You can see that in the history of the twentieth-century church, in the divisions between **Pentecostals** and charismatics on the one hand and most mainstream denominations on the other (although the first two decades of this century have seen a lot of encouraging developments on both sides). Division was there in the first-century church too. Some believers at Corinth thought their spiritual gifts made them inferior to others (**v 15-20**). Some thought their spiritual gifts made them superior to others (**v 21-26**). And presumably, since this is what usually happens when churches squabble about things, everyone else got caught in the crossfire. For those of us who have experienced painful disagreements on this subject, this section is a goldmine of pastoral and theological wisdom.

The main point of the section is stated simply at the start: "Just as a body, though one, has many parts, but all its many parts form one body, so it is with Christ" (**v 12**). Bodies are a magnificent metaphor for the church because they express unity-in-diversity like nothing else on earth. The body is one, not in spite of the fact that it has many different parts which all have different functions but because of it. Oneness is only possible because of many-ness. Unity is only possible with diversity. So it is not surprising that the same is true of the body of Christ, the church.

The next two sentences provide the rationale for our unity-in-diversity, in a pair of neatly matched opposites: many have become one (**v 13**), but the one remains many (**v 14**). The grounds for knowing that many have become one, for Paul, are our shared experience of the Spirit. All of us, whatever our ethnicity (Jew or Gentile) or station in life (slave or free), were baptised in one Spirit into one body. All of us were given one Spirit to drink (**v 13**). That shared experience of the Holy Spirit—Paul expresses it with strikingly experiential language, using the words *baptizo* (drench, plunge, immerse) and *potizo* (water, give to drink)—has turned many into one. The modern idea that some Christians have drunk from and been drenched in the Spirit and others have not is not just foreign to Paul's argument here; it is in direct opposition to it.

Yet while many have become one, the one remains many (**v 14**). Our unity has not destroyed our diversity. Rather, our oneness depends on our many-ness. All of us have different gifts, and the body will only flourish to the extent that all of us use them for the benefit of the whole—which, as Paul points out in the next two paragraphs, is exactly how the human body works. The body needs hands and feet, ears and eyes, and dozens of other organs that make vitally different contributions (**v 15-16**). If you were all eye, or all hand, you would not be a body; you would be a freakshow (**v 17**). In the same way, if everyone was a teacher or a miracle-worker but nobody was prophesying or helping, you wouldn't have a church; you would have a madhouse. Bodies, and churches, only thrive when the full range of their members is recognised, released and celebrated. Interdependence is built in. God has designed us that way (**v 18-20**).

This has two implications which Paul wants to press home to the Corinthians and to us. The first is that nobody should dismiss their own gift (**v 15-16**). I have done this myself on many occasions: comparing myself with other people, wishing I had the gifts that God has given them, and concluding that mine really aren't very important or exciting. ("Anybody can read books and teach people," I have muttered to myself, "but healing someone or working miracles takes a real spiritual gift".) *Bunk,* Paul says. Ears cannot see. Eyes cannot hear. People with other gifts need you, just as you need them. "God has placed the parts in the body, every one of them, just as he wanted them to be" (**v 18**).

The second implication is that nobody should dismiss the gifts of other people. Some Corinthians, it appears, were saying (or thinking) about other church members, "I don't need you!" (**v 21**). We Christians today, in our pride, are tempted to do the same thing, prizing our gifts as more important than the gifts of others and looking down on believers who are less

> Nobody should dismiss their own gift. People with other gifts need you, just as you need them.

gifted in teaching, leading, healing, serving, prophesying or whatever. This, Paul says, is like an eye thinking it no longer needs a hand, not considering what will happen when it next gets an eyelash stuck. Heads might think that they are more important than feet, but if they think they can get by without them, heads will roll.

A true understanding of the body will produce humility. If we prioritise what is visible and impressive (preaching, prophesying), and demean what is invisible (helping, praying), we should remember that the truly indispensable parts of our bodies are the ones we don't think about (**v 22**). You can survive without an eye or a hand, but not without a liver. If anything, the fact that a body part is hidden away as unpresentable—Paul is talking about sexual organs here—is a sign of how special it is (**v 23**), and in the same way God has given "greater honour to the parts that lacked it" (**v 24**). So there should be no superiority, no smugness and no self-pity; every member is needed, and the suffering or honour of even the smallest member becomes the suffering or honour of the whole body (**v 26**). Most of all, "there should be no division in the body, but ... its parts should have equal concern for each other" (**v 25**).

Questions for reflection

1. How has this passage honed or changed your view of spiritual gifts and their use?

2. What gifts has God given you? How will you use those gifts to benefit others?

3. Which fellow-believers are you tempted to look down on? What would it look like for you to have concern for them instead?

PART TWO

The Body in Action

In the final section of chapter 12 Paul applies his picture of the church as a body to the Corinthian situation. Interestingly, and unusually for Paul, he has developed an extended metaphor for fifteen verses straight, talking about the human body without once making explicit that he is really talking about spiritual gifts in the church (**v 14-26**). Finally, for those who might have missed it, he makes it clear: "Now you are the body of Christ, and each one of you is a part of it" (**v 27**).

If we have been following the body metaphor through the chapter, we will be expecting a classically democratic conclusion (at least we will if we are Western readers). Every gift is as important as every other. No part of the body is more vital than any other. You are all equal. As the Queen of Hearts puts it in *Alice in Wonderland*, "All must have prizes".

But Paul has a surprise for us. On the one hand, he remains absolutely clear on the interdependence of the body, our need for each other, and the fact that nobody can thrive without drawing on the gifts of everyone else. Nobody has everything, but everybody has something: "Are all apostles? Are all prophets? Are all teachers? Do all work miracles? Do all have gifts of healing? Do all speak in tongues? Do all interpret?" (**v 29-30**). Churches, and even denominations, can look to make their gift of choice a test of real spirituality, whether it be teaching (in more conservative churches) or tongue-speaking (in more Pentecostal ones). But Paul is as clear as he can be: there is no gift that is common to everybody. That's the whole point of the body.

On the other hand, Paul also believes that some gifts take precedence over others. He urges them to "eagerly desire the greater gifts" (**v 31**), and puts several of the gifts in order: "first of all apostles, second prophets, third teachers, then miracles, then gifts of healing, of helping, of guidance, and of different kinds of tongues" (**v 28**). At one level, this simply reflects the reality of what bodies are like: all parts are equally valuable and equally part of the body, but there are some that you simply cannot live without (a heart, a brain) and some that you can (an ear, a leg). At another level, we can see Paul preparing the ground for the argument he will make in chapter 14.

In **12:28-30** he does this in several subtle ways. He puts apostles first, which both provides a gentle reminder of his authority to correct them on these matters and adds another intriguing layer to the "apostles first" and "apostles last" back-and-forth that has been building throughout the letter (3:5-10; 4:8-13, 14-15; 9:1-2, 19-23; **12:28**; 15:9-10). He puts prophets second, which gets us ready for the command to pursue prophecy "eagerly" and "especially" in 14:1. (Here Paul is clearly not referring to the Old Testament prophets, since he is speaking of gifts that exist within the Corinthian church.) He puts teachers third, which may or may not have bothered the Corinthians but sometimes bothers the sorts of teachers who write **commentaries**. He then lists four gifts without numbering them, mixing ones that might seem very impressive and dramatic (miracles and healings) with ones that might seem more ordinary and everyday (helping and *kubernesis*, which is often translated "administration" but referred to the guiding role of a helmsman on a ship). And most significantly for his subsequent argument, he puts the gift with which the Corinthians were most obsessed, namely tongue-speaking, last. The stage is set, after a chapter of teaching on the gifts in general, for Paul to bring some more specific application to the way they are to be used in corporate worship.

Before doing that, however, Paul wants to ensure that the motive for using the gifts—and in fact the motive for everything we do in the Christian life—is properly established. Spiritual gifts are wonderful, but there is a "more excellent way" (**12:31**). It leads him to write the most famous chapter in Scripture, and one of the most powerful in all literature.

The Priority of Love

The words of **13:1-13** have been read billions of times: privately and publicly, on radio and television, in churches and on film, by people who follow Jesus and people who don't. They risk becoming domesticated, or even meaningless, through overfamiliarity. Yet I wonder how many people who hear them, or even read them aloud at weddings, know why they talk about "the tongues of men or of angels" and "the gift of prophecy" and "all mysteries and all knowledge" and "faith that can move mountains" (**v 1-2**) or have any idea that they were originally written about spiritual gifts. Not many, I suspect.

We had hints of this in chapter 12, and we will see it more fully explained in chapter 14, but this section indicates that the Corinthians were being loveless in their use of spiritual gifts. Some of them thought of tongue-speaking, whether in human or angelic languages, as valuable in itself; Paul sees it as empty noise without love (**13:1**). Others revelled in prophecy, insight, knowledge and miraculous levels of faith; Paul saw them as nothing without love (**v 2**). Others emphasised more sacrificial gifts, like giving up all of your possessions, your comfort, or even your life; Paul dismissed them as worthless without love (**v 3**). No matter whether we tend towards the **fundamentalist**, excitable Right or the liberal, do-gooding Left, our hallmarks of spirituality are put firmly in their place here. All you need is love.

What people mean by "love", of course, varies dramatically. In contemporary Western culture the word is often used romantically and/or erotically—the Summer of Love, love songs, *Love Island*, and so forth—as if it refers to an intense feeling of sexualised affection for someone. Few of us use "love" to describe even close friendships, and we are more likely to use it about ice cream than a colleague. If you search for "love" on Google images, you will get a flurry of red hearts and Valentine's flowers but precious few parents with their children and even fewer pictures of Christ on the cross. For most of the people in our communities, "love" evokes sex and sentimentality more than steadfastness and sacrifice.

Paul does not want the Corinthians, or us, to lose the power of this most fundamental Christian word to a mushy vagueness. So he tells us—as if to anticipate the questions of Whitesnake, Bob Marley, Foreigner, Haddaway, S Club 7 and many others—exactly what love is, using fifteen different qualities. As he does so, it is hard to miss the way in which his definition has been shaped by the person and work of Jesus Christ.

> Paul does not want us to lose the power of the word "love" to a mushy vagueness.

Seven of the fifteen, topping and tailing the list, tell us what love is, as opposed to what it is not. Love is patient and kind (**v 4**). It rejoices with the truth (**v 6**). It always protects, always trusts, always hopes, always perseveres (**v 7**). It is striking that Paul here defines what in Galatians 5:22-23 he lists as the first part of the fruit of the Spirit (love) with reference to several of the others (joy, patience, kindness, goodness, faithfulness, self-control). When we are praying for others, it can be helpful to take these seven qualities and ask God to help us express that kind of love—ever-hopeful, ever-protecting, ever-patient, and so on—to our friends, family, colleagues or fellow church members.

The other eight qualities tell us what love is not. It is not envious, boastful, proud, dishonouring, self-seeking or easily angered; it does not keep a record of wrongs or delight in evil (1 Corinthians **13:5-6**). Again, it can be beneficial to audit our relationships in the light of that list. Am I envious of my colleagues? Dishonouring of my husband or wife? Easily angered by my children? Keeping a record of my parents' wrongs? Delighting in evil with my friends? Lord, help me to love!

In context, though, these searching and beautiful words are primarily designed to help churches use spiritual gifts wisely. I am sure Paul would be thrilled (if a little surprised) to have heard that people would be reading his words at weddings 2,000 years later. But his intention was that nobody elevate prophesying over patience, healing over hope, speaking in languages over speaking in love. If I do that, however spiritual I might feel about it, "I am nothing" (**v 2**).

The Permanence of Love

In several ways, Paul's teaching on spiritual gifts (chapters 12 – 14) runs parallel to his teaching about idol food (chapters 8 – 10). Both sections start with a chapter that addresses the issue more generally and theologically (chapters 8 and 12), and finish with a chapter that makes more specific application to the various scenarios and problems in the church (chapters 10 and 14). In the middle sits a chapter in which Paul focuses on the heart behind his teaching: the fact that our love for others is more important than our freedom to eat whatever we want (chapter 9) or use whatever gifts we want (chapter 13). In both cases he uses himself as an example and builds towards a conclusion that focuses on our future hope together (9:24-27; **13:8-13**).

The reason he does that here in chapter 13 is to draw a very specific contrast, which adds weight to his insistence that love should take precedence over use of the gifts. Spiritual gifts, he explains, will all cease (**v 8**). Prophecies will end. Languages will be silenced. "Knowledge"—at least in the partial, finite, limited sense that the Corinthians talk about it—will pass away. But "love never fails". Love is permanent and will outlive all the gifts that the Corinthians get so excited about. As such, it should surely take priority over them in the meantime.

Spiritual gifts are not just temporary. They are also partial and incomplete. We know and we prophesy "in part" (**v 9**), with partial knowledge and incomplete prophecy (a point which is important to bear in mind when thinking about the practice of prophecy, both then and now). Ultimately, what is partial will fade into the background and disappear "when completeness comes" (**v 10**). That is how maturity works. It is all very well talking and acting like children when you are a child because that is the way that things are supposed to work. But when you become an adult, you put childish talk behind you and behave like an adult (**v 11**). *In the same way,* Paul explains, *I have knowledge and languages and prophesying for now, but the day is coming when I will no longer need them, because I will have reached maturity and will "know fully, even as I am fully known" (***v 12***).*

An important question to ask at this point is: when? If spiritual gifts like these will cease, and Paul is very clear that they will, then when will that happen? The history of the church has thrown up a range of answers, including after the death of the last apostle (around AD 100) and after the finalisation of the **canon** of Scripture (around AD 400)— and if prophecy and languages and knowledge all ceased a long time ago, then they are not available to us today, and Paul's instructions to pursue them (**12:31**; 14:1) no longer apply to us.

This is not Paul's view, however. He talks about the cessation of these gifts as taking place "when completeness comes" (**13:10**), when we see "face to face" as opposed to "only a reflection as in a mirror," and when we know "fully" as opposed to "in part" (**v 12**). As virtually all commentators agree, Paul is not talking about the death of the last apostle or the finalisation of the Bible here; his future hope simply does not work that way, in this letter or anywhere else, and at a historical level it would be hard to argue that the church has experienced completion and fullness of knowledge since the fifth century. Language like this can only refer to the return of Christ and the renewal of all things, when all things will be completed and we will see Jesus face to face. On that day, the partial and temporary—prophecy, teaching, languages, knowledge, healing and so forth—will pass away because they will no longer be needed, like stars fading into the background in the light of the rising sun.

"And now these three remain: faith, hope and love" (**v 13**). Paul might mean, as some interpreters have argued, that love will remain for ever while faith and hope only remain for "now", because they will turn to sight in the presence of Christ. Personally I don't think Paul is making that point, given his reference to the fact that love "always trusts, always hopes" (**v 7**); the nature of all three will change at the return of Christ, but eternity will be faithful and hopeful just as it will be loving. Instead, I think that Paul is balancing the triad of things which cease (prophecy, languages and knowledge) with a triad of things which remain (faith, hope and love), using a combination of virtues that he often groups together. Even so, given his wider argument in these chapters, it is not surprising that he still sees one of them as more important than the others: "the greatest of these is love" (**v 13**). *And,* he challenges the Corinthians, *so should you see it like that.* So should we.

Questions for reflection

1. Which spiritual gifts do you "eagerly desire" and why? Does anything need to change?

2. Think through your average week. How can you make sure that you prioritise love over all things?

3. Reread these verses replacing "love" and "it" with "Christ". How does this prompt you to worship him?

10. EAGERLY DESIRE SPIRITUAL GIFTS

"Follow the way of love and eagerly desire gifts of the Spirit, especially prophecy" (**14:1**). This is one of three exhortations to pursue prophecy in 1 Corinthians (12:31; **14:39**), and similar instructions occur in two of Paul's other letters (Romans 12:6; 1 Thessalonians 5:19-21). Yet although we are urged to desire the gift of prophecy on five different occasions in three different letters—including here, where it is clearly the main point of an entire chapter—many Christians in the Western world today would never dream of actually doing so. (Things are different in the **majority world**, for a variety of reasons which we don't have space to get into now.)

Why? What is it that makes so many Christians who read the Bible carefully and take it very seriously conclude that this particular instruction does not apply? It is worth considering that question at the start of this chapter, because the whole passage is all about how to use the gifts of prophecy and languages, and therefore we will miss the point of it if we don't know whether it is applicable to us. I take the view (spoiler alert) that Paul's instructions do apply to us, and that all Christians should desire and use the gift of prophecy. But since many do not, it is worth summarising why they do not, and why I disagree (I have written on this subject at much more length in my book *Spirit and Sacrament*.) Their argument runs something like this:

1. Prophecy in the Old Testament was revelatory, foundational and **infallible**.

2. New Testament prophecy is no different.

3. With the death of the apostles and the completion of the New Testament, this kind of foundational, infallible revelation has stopped being given. We should not expect any new inspired texts or papal decrees or modern revelations that carry infallible divine weight like the Bible does.

4. Therefore the gift of prophecy has ceased.

5. Therefore the gift of languages, which functions very much like prophecy in 1 Corinthians 14, has also ceased.

6. In many (although not all) versions of the argument, healing and miracles—which are given to confirm the validity of the message when it is first proclaimed—have ceased as well.

The best defence of this "cessationist position" that I have come across is given by Tom Schreiner in *Spiritual Gifts: What They Are and Why They Matter*. And it sounds quite plausible. But there are problems with five of those six points:

1. There are lots of examples in the Old Testament where the language of "prophets" and "prophesying" does not refer to infallible, foundational divine revelation, or in fact revelatory speech at all (for example, Genesis 20:7; Numbers 11:25-29; 1 Samuel 10:6; 19:20-23; 1 Kings 18:4; 2 Kings 2:3; 4:38; 6:1; 9:1; 17:13; 1 Chronicles 25:1-3; 29:29; 2 Chronicles 9:29; 12:15; 13:22).

2. It is far from clear that all prophecy in the New Testament is like this either. The current chapter describes prophecy being used to encourage, console and edify other believers in the local church (1 Corinthians **14:3**), bring unbelievers under conviction (**v 24**), witness to the presence of the Holy Spirit in the assembly (**v 25**), and enable the congregation to learn and be encouraged (**v 31**). There seems to be a big difference between the prophecy Paul is talking about in this chapter—where numerous Corinthian prophets are chipping in (and therefore having to be limited to two or three per meeting), often talking over each other, needing their prophecies to be weighed by those sitting down, and never

recording it or transmitting it to another church—and the kind we see in the ministry of Isaiah, for instance.

3. This point is clearly true: we should not expect any further infallible divine speech beyond what is revealed in Christ and in Scripture.

4. But although there is no more Isaiah-like prophecy, there is no reason to think that Corinth-like prophecy has ceased, let alone…

5. … that the gift of languages at Corinth conveyed infallible divine revelation, as we will see.

6. Nor is there any reason to think that healings and miracles were only given to confirm the apostles' message, and therefore would serve no function once the Bible was completed. We have already heard Paul say that they are "for the common good" (12:7) and the care of the whole body (12:24-25), and of course they are given to make sick people better (James 5:14-15).

As a rule, we are better off assuming that New Testament passages (including this one) apply to us, unless there is a clear indication from the context that they do not, and that their instructions should be obeyed. In this case, there is no indication like that; if anything, as we have seen, Paul seems to teach that prophecy and the rest of the gifts will continue until the return of Christ (1 Corinthians 13:8-13). So for the rest of this chapter, I am going to assume that Paul is urging you and me, as well as the Corinthians, to eagerly desire spiritual gifts and especially prophecy. To do that, we need to understand what prophecy is.

What Is Prophecy?

Paul's purpose in this chapter is to commend the gift of prophecy, and particularly to commend it as more useful in public contexts than the gift of languages. By all accounts the Corinthians were obsessed with languages—it is hard to make sense of **14:1-25** otherwise—and

Paul wants to reorder their preferences so that they prioritise prophecy above languages. In the opening paragraph, he presents two contrasts to show them why they should. He will expand on both as the chapter continues.

The first contrast is that prophecy, unlike tongue-speaking, involves speaking "to people for their strengthening, encouraging and comfort" (**v 3**). When we prophesy, we are directing our speech towards other human beings, who can understand us and be strengthened by what we are saying. Whoever speaks in tongues, on the other hand, "does not speak to people but to God" (**v 2**). This might be because all tongue-speaking is directed to God (like prayer) rather than to people (like prophecy); or it might be because people cannot understand the language, whereas God can. Either way, when people speak in tongues without interpretation, "no one understands them; they utter mysteries by the Spirit". What you don't understand is unlikely to make you stronger. That makes prophecy a more useful gift for public gatherings.

The second contrast brings a different angle: "Anyone who speaks in a tongue edifies themselves, but the one who prophesies edifies the church" (**v 4**). When I speak in languages, I am building up myself. (I am doing it while writing this chapter, for exactly that reason.) Speaking in tongues fortifies the individual who is speaking. But unless it is interpreted, it doesn't fortify anyone else. Prophecy is different, however. It edifies the church. It strengthens people in faith. So if I want to use my gift for the edification of the church rather than myself, I should seek to prophesy rather than speak in languages. Paul loves the gift of tongues and would like everybody in the church to use it, but he would rather they all prophesied. He even goes so far as to say that the prophet is "greater" than the one who speaks in uninterpreted languages (**v 5**), echoing the provocative hierarchy of gifts he presented earlier (12:28).

As such, the opening paragraph gives a very simple message: prefer prophecy to languages because people (not just God) will understand what you're saying and fellow church members (not just you) will be strengthened by it. But it also gives us a very helpful start when it comes to understanding what prophecy is, at least in the context of this letter. Prophetic speech is directed towards people, and it strengthens, encourages and comforts us.

The rest of the chapter fills out the picture. Prophecy is spoken of as "revelation" (**14:6, 26, 30**), which has the capacity to convict unbelievers of sin (**v 24**) and lay bare the secrets of their hearts, so that they recognise the presence of God among the church (**v 25**). It exists so that the church may be built up (**v 26**). It must be weighed by others (**v 29**), which is not surprising given that we already know that it is partial rather than perfect (13:9). It can be spontaneous but need not be (**14:30**). And it is something which all of us should pursue (**v 1, 39**), even though ultimately it is not given to everyone (12:10, 28-29). In an excellent definition, which is often quoted in commentaries on this passage, Anthony Thiselton summarises it like this:

"Prophecy, as a gift of the Holy Spirit, combines pastoral insight into the needs of persons, communities, and situations with the ability to address these with a God-given utterance or longer discourse (whether unprompted or prepared with judgment, decision and rational reflection) leading to challenge or comfort, judgment, or consolation, but ultimately building up the addressees . . . While the speaker believes that such utterances or discourses come from the Holy Spirit, mistakes can be made, and since believers, including ministers or prophets, remain humanly fallible, claims to prophecy must be weighed and tested."

(*The First Epistle to the Corinthians*, page 965; see also David Garland, *1 Corinthians*, page 583; Roy Ciampa and Brian Rosner, *The First Letter to the Corinthians*, page 581)

Paul will have more to say on the use of the gift in due course. For now, though, this will help us make sense of exactly what he is talking about and why we should prize it so highly.

How (Not) to Speak in Languages

After an opening paragraph in which he has commended prophecy ahead of tongue-speaking, Paul spends the next fourteen verses talking about how to speak (and how not to speak) in languages, before moving on to prophecy in the second half of the chapter. As we read through the next couple of paragraphs, it is important to remember that Paul's problem is not with the gift of languages in itself; as he reminds the Corinthians, he speaks in tongues more than all of them (**14:18**). His problem is with the self-indulgent use of languages in public meetings, without interpretation, without any regard for unbelievers and without consideration for the rest of the church. We are beginning to see why he spent so long talking about love (13:1-13) before addressing the use of this specific gift.

Paul is blunt: *If I come to you and speak in tongues, and I don't bring "some revelation or knowledge or prophecy or word of instruction", then I will do you no good whatsoever* (**14:6**). (The three terms listed with "prophecy" here overlap with one another, and together they summarise the various sorts of comprehensible public speech.) A person burbling away in tongues in a public meeting, without interpretation, doesn't edify anyone; they are as much use as a harp in which all the notes are the same (**v 7**) or a trumpet which sounds like blowing a raspberry rather than a clear call to battle (**v 8**). Charismatic and Pentecostal churches, like the ones to which I have belonged for my entire adult life, need to be reminded of this (especially, in my experience, when it comes to singing). The purpose of a gift in the gathered church is to edify people, not to parade our spirituality, and gifts can't be edifying if they aren't intel-

> The purpose of a gift in the gathered church is to edify people, not to parade our spirituality.

ligible. You might be having a great time, but if nobody understands a word you're saying, "you will just be speaking into the air" (**v 9**).

So far I have translated *glossa* with a combination of "language" and "tongue". Most of our English translations go for "tongues", but that can sound either old-fashioned or a bit spooky, so I usually prefer "languages"; *glossa* is the normal word you would use for English, Mandarin, Swahili and so on. For Paul, in fact, the reality that the Corinthians are speaking a language (as opposed to a sequence of nonsensical noises) is actually very important. His argument runs like this: the world is full of languages, and they all mean something, and the whole point of speaking them is to be understood (**v 10-11**). It is the same with you when you use this gift in the congregation. You are all eager for spiritual gifts, and rightly so. But "try to excel in those that build up the church" (**v 12**).

So far, it might sound as if Paul is issuing a blanket ban on speaking in languages in the gathered church, and many congregations have taken it that way. If so, we need to read on. Paul's application is not that the Corinthians should ban tongue-speaking—later he will explicitly tell them not to ban it (**v 39**)—but that "the one who speaks in a tongue should pray that they may interpret what they say" (**v 13**). The problem is not with languages but with uninterpreted languages that edify nobody. So if you are going to speak in languages in a public meeting, you should pray that you might interpret what you are saying. It will benefit you, by enabling you to pray with your mind as well as your spirit, rather than leaving your mind unfruitful (**v 14-15**). It will also benefit others, by enabling them to say "Amen" to your prayer, rather than wondering what on earth you were talking about (**v 16**). Despite the practice in some churches of shouting out in tongues and leaving the interpretation to someone else, Paul says it is our responsibility, when we speak in languages, to interpret what we have said (unless we know there is someone else around who can interpret)—and if we aren't going to do that, we should keep quiet (**v 28**). Otherwise, though you may be giving thanks yourself, nobody else is getting any stronger (**v 17**).

For all this, Paul loves speaking in languages privately: "I thank God that I speak in tongues more than all of you" (**v 18**). It is a gift of the Spirit; it edifies him; it expresses prayer and thanksgiving to God; and it may even articulate the wordless prayers of the Spirit that Paul talks about elsewhere (Romans 8:26-27). Nevertheless, when we are gathered together as a church, it is better to speak five words that other people can make sense of and profit from than ten thousand words that they can't (1 Corinthians **14:19**). Love for others, as we have seen so many times in this letter, trumps my right to express myself.

Questions for reflection

1. What is your experience of differing views on prophecy and tongues? Does this chapter challenge your assumptions, and how? If so, who could you discuss this with?

2. Do you think you have ever exercised the gift of prophecy? How could you pursue it more?

3. Do your words generally build up and edify others?

PART TWO

Spiritual Gifts and Unbelievers

14:20-25 is one of the trickiest passages in the letter because at first glance it looks as if Paul is completely contradicting himself. One minute he is saying that tongues is a sign for unbelievers and prophecy is for believers (**v 22**). The next minute he appears to be saying the exact opposite: if unbelievers hear prophecy, it will bring them to repentance and worship, whereas if they hear people speaking in languages, they will think those people are all crazy (**v 23-25**). Common sense suggests that the second of these is true—prophetic revelation is much more likely than tongue-speaking to evoke worship from an unbeliever—as well as much more in line with Paul's argument so far about languages, prophecy and intelligibility. But in that case, what does he mean when he says that tongues is a sign for unbelievers? What is going on here?

Paul's goal in this paragraph is simple: he wants the Corinthians to grow up. Having a childlike innocence with respect to evil is a good thing, but in their thinking they need to stop being children and start being adults (**v 20**). The child/adult comparison has already appeared twice in this letter (4:14; 13:11), and in the second of these it contrasted maturity with immaturity, which is what it does here. By running after the gift of languages without regard for the edification or understanding of anyone else, the Corinthians are being childish, like a toddler so obsessed with enjoying their toys that they never think about anyone else.

Then comes the quotation from the Old Testament (Paul sometimes says "the Law" to refer to the Hebrew Scriptures as a whole) which makes sense of what Paul is doing (**14:21**). It comes from Isaiah 28:11-12, which is a passage pronouncing judgment over unbelieving Israel, from seven centuries before. Because of Israel's sin, Isaiah says, God will judge them by speaking to them through foreigners who will rule over them—Assyrians, then Babylonians, then Persians and eventually Greeks and Romans—in languages that they do not understand. Prophecy, meanwhile, will reassure them of God's continued presence among them, not least through Isaiah's own words.

So when Paul says that "tongues, then, are a sign, not for believers but for unbelievers" (1 Corinthians **14:22**), he is talking about a sign of judgment. He is saying that the experience of being spoken to in languages you do not understand serves to emphasise your distance from God, as it did for Israel. It creates a sense of alienation in the hearer—in contrast to prophecy, which emphasises how present God is. So by speaking in uninterpreted tongues in the church, the Corinthians are (unintentionally) pronouncing judgment over one another. They are making people feel further away from God, and from each other, rather than closer. If you have ever been in a meeting where everyone is speaking in tongues and you don't, you may know what that feels like.

A clue that we are on the right lines here is the word "so" (*oun*) at the start of **verse 23**. If we take the phrase "a sign for unbelievers" as a good thing which we should embrace, then that little word "so" makes no sense: Paul is saying completely different things in the two sentences. But if we take "a sign for unbelievers" as a sign of judgment which we should avoid if at all possible, it makes perfect sense. Both verses are trying to prevent the Corinthians babbling away in languages that nobody understands, because it will make Christians feel judged by God and alienated from one another (**v 22**), and because it will make unbelievers think the Christians are all crazy (**v 23**). Prophecy, on the other hand, is edifying to believers (**v 3, 5**) and has the capacity to convince unbelievers of their sin, expose the secrets of their hearts, reveal the presence of God, and cause them to fall face down in worship (**v 24-25**).

Church history is full of examples, but one of my favourites comes from the life of Charles Spurgeon:

"Mr. Spurgeon looked at me as if he knew me, and in his sermon he pointed to me, and told the congregation that I was a shoemaker, and that I kept my shop open on Sundays; and I did, sir. I should not have minded that; but he also said that I took ninepence the Sunday before, and that there was fourpence profit out of it. I did take ninepence that day, and fourpence was just the profit; but how he should know that, I could not tell. Then it struck me that it was God who had spoken to my soul though him, so I shut up my shop the next Sunday. At first, I was afraid to go again to hear him, lest he should tell the people more about me; but afterwards I went, and the Lord met with me, and saved my soul."

(*The Autobiography of Charles H. Spurgeon*, 2:226-27)

Spiritual gifts are not just given to strengthen the church but to reveal the presence and holiness of God to unbelievers. It is a wonderful privilege.

Practising the Gifts

Verses 26-33 provide the practical application of the chapter. Until now, Paul has primarily been establishing the principle rather than the practice: we should pursue prophecy rather than uninterpreted languages because prophecy strengthens believers and reveals God to unbelievers. Here, he describes what that ought to look like in the context of a Christian meeting. His teaching is obviously relevant for other contexts as well, but we should remember that his focus throughout these chapters is on what happens when the church gathers publicly (**v 23, 26**).

"What then shall we say, brothers and sisters? When you come together, each of you has a hymn, or a word of instruction, a revelation, a tongue or an interpretation" (**v 26**). That statement reveals a huge amount about early Christian worship. The church is a body, and everyone has been given spiritual gifts for the common good (12:4-10). Gifts do not reside with a pastor or vicar, or a group of elders or deacons, or men, or a small coterie of individuals who have been believers for a long time; they belong to everyone. So Corinthian worship, unlike that of many churches today, involved contributions from all sorts of people. One person might bring a song, another a teaching (the word *didache* is the usual word for teaching or doctrine), another a prophecy, or a language, or an interpretation. Worship was not a spectator sport. The practice of spiritual gifts, like the Eucharist itself, was more like a bring-and-share lunch than a formal dinner.

To some of us that sounds like paradise; to others it sounds like mayhem. Whichever way we lean, Paul's next statement is critical: "Everything must be done so that the church may be built up" (**14:26**). Some churches, like the one in Corinth, had taken the fact that they all had spiritual gifts as a licence to express those gifts in corporate worship whether or not they were useful or encouraging to everyone else (the "if you've got it, flaunt it" approach). This, to put it mildly, was not Paul's view. If the gifts are given for the common good, then they, and we, should only speak publicly in a meeting in order to strengthen, encourage and build up other people.

For many of us that will mean keeping quiet. Paul wants the whole church to speak in languages (**v 5**), but he only wants two or three to speak in languages in a meeting—and there must always be an interpretation (**v 27**), and if there isn't, then the tongue-speaker should stay quiet (**v 28**). Paul wants the whole church to be able to prophesy (**v 5**), but he only wants two or three prophets to speak in one service—and people must weigh carefully what is said (**v 29**), and if someone else starts prophesying, then the speaker should stop (**v 30**). In a church with at least fifty members, and possibly quite a few more, that means that the vast majority will say nothing: not because we do not have gifts to use, but because our goal is edification, not self-expression.

Paul does not elaborate here on how to "weigh" or discern a prophecy. Based on his teaching in these chapters, we can assume it would involve considering how it lines up with Scripture, whether it exalts Jesus as Lord, and whether it edifies the body. But however it happens, weighing is vital. To accept all revelations as equally weighty, without discernment, does not indicate a higher view of prophecy but a lower one—a point Paul makes elsewhere: "Do not quench the Spirit. Do not treat prophecies with contempt but test them all; hold on to what is good, reject every kind of evil" (1 Thessalonians 5:19-22). Eat the fish, and spit out the bones.

This process is important, and it is also possible. Prophesying is not an ecstatic, out-of-body experience in which the speaker has no control over their body or their speech: "the spirits of prophets are subject to the control of prophets" (1 Corinthians **14:32**). Anyone who claims to be forced to prophesy, or says that they cannot help speaking in languages, is not speaking by the Spirit. So it is perfectly possible for people to "prophesy in turn so that everyone may be instructed and encouraged" (**v 31**). **Charismata** should never lead to chaos, despite the excesses we occasionally hear about or see on television, and when handled wisely—which happens far more often but rarely gets shown on television—they don't. "For God is not a God of disorder but of peace—as in all the congregations of the Lord's people" (**v 33**). The same God who gives gifts provides peace.

> Charismata should never lead to chaos, and when handled wisely they don't.

A Final Puzzle

There are various parts of the Bible, and of Paul's letters, about which people say, "Surely it can't mean *that*". Usually, that is because we don't like it. We read something that doesn't fit with our modern sensibilities, so we do a huge amount of **exegetical** work to try and make it look as if it means something else. (Scholars who are not Christians can be a huge help here. Because they don't claim to obey Scripture, they are sometimes better at admitting what it actually says.) But occasionally, the "surely it can't mean that" reflex is based on the text itself. Something in the passage, or the book as a whole, makes it clear that the obvious interpretation is not actually correct. Nowhere is this truer than of Paul's statement in **verse 34**: "Women should remain silent in the churches. They are not allowed to speak, but must be in submission, as the law says".

It sounds like an absolute ban on women speaking in the church service. But this cannot be what Paul means. He recently spent fifteen verses on the question of what women should wear over their heads while praying or prophesying in the church service (11:2-16), which would make no sense whatsoever if women were prohibited from public speech. He has also spent much of the last few chapters explaining how "each one" in the congregation has a gift, and how "each one" can and should use it—whether in songs, teaching, prophecy, languages or interpretation—for the edification of the body (**14:26**). So he cannot mean that women are not allowed to speak at all. Unless we are to conclude that Paul did not write these verses at all (and these verses appear in all the manuscripts we have), he must mean something else.

The two most plausible explanations are these. One: Paul is prohibiting women from the weighing of prophecy (**v 29-30**) because it involves a governmental responsibility that Paul limits to the fathers of the church (the elders, the overseers, or whatever we call them). Two: some women at Corinth were in the habit of interrupting their husbands while they were prophesying, asking questions and bringing shame on themselves in the process, and Paul will not allow this because it is not submissive or honourable, and it leads to disorder rather than peace. In either scenario, the requirement of wives to be submissive "as the law says" is probably a reference to Genesis, whether the creation story (as in 1 Corinthians 11:7-9; see 1 Timothy 2:13-14) or the patriarchal stories (see 1 Peter 3:5-6). Personally I take the second view on the interpretation of 1 Corinthians **14:34**, which fits well with the next sentence: "If they want to enquire about something, they should ask their own husbands at home; for it is disgraceful for a woman to speak in the church" (**v 35**). But it is difficult to be sure.

In the final few verses of the chapter, Paul reinforces his teaching on prophecy and languages with a strong rhetorical appeal (**v 36-38**), followed by a summarising conclusion (**v 39-40**). The rhetorical appeal contains several elements that are familiar to us by now. The gospel did not originate with the Corinthians (**v 36**). They received it from Paul—a point he has made before and will make again (3:5-6, 10-11; 4:15; 15:1-2). Nor are they the only ones it has reached (**14:36**); again, Paul has appealed to the practice of other churches to bring the Corinthians into line (see 11:16). So no matter how prophetic or spiritually gifted the Corinthians may think they are, they cannot simply do their own thing here; it is a command of the Lord himself (**14:37**), and anyone who ignores it will be ignored themselves (**v 38**). Prophecy is a wonderful gift, which Paul has celebrated throughout this chapter, but it should never lead to anyone setting aside the law (**v 34**), the gospel (**v 36**), or Jesus' commands through his apostles (**v 37**).

In conclusion, then, we should "be eager to prophesy, and ... not forbid speaking in tongues. But everything should be done in a fitting and orderly way" (**v 39-40**). These two statements not only provide a crisp summary of chapter 14, but they also provide a striking challenge to both the charismatic and **conservative** sections of the global church. Conservatives need to hear that prophecy should be pursued and that languages should not be forbidden. Charismatics need to hear that everything should be done in a fitting and orderly way, with a focus on comprehensibility, edification and the lordship of Christ. May Paul's instructions here bring unity as well as wisdom to the church of Christ.

Questions for reflection

1. Have you ever felt alienated by what people say or do in a church meeting? How can you learn from that experience in what you yourself say and do?

2. Think about times when you have spoken in a Christian gathering. What was your motivation? Do you think you should speak more, or less, or differently, in future?

3. As you reflect on chapter 14, what will you pray for your church?

11. CHRIST HAS BEEN RAISED

Every few years, it seems to me, evangelicals have a debate about how to define the gospel. The gospel, some insist, is all about the kingdom of God. Yes, others respond, but it must include the **substitutionary** death of Jesus for our sins. Yes, but it centres on the resurrection and the inauguration of a new world. Yes, but if it doesn't show individuals how to be saved, then it isn't a gospel. As the discussion goes round and round, it gets more heated. "Your gospel has so much justification that there is no space for justice." "Your gospel doesn't sound like good news at all." It carries on like this for a while, until someone with enough credit in the bank on both sides steps in and says, "Can't it be both?" At which point everyone calms down for a while, until a few years later it all starts again.

In all this back-and-forth about what the gospel is, however, one thing that virtually everyone agrees on is that this letter, and this chapter in particular, and this section of this chapter above all, are at the heart of it. Paul says so himself: "Now, brothers and sisters, I want to remind you of the gospel I preached to you, which you received and on which you have taken your stand" (**15:1**). Admittedly, Paul talks about the gospel all the time and summarises it in a variety of different ways in his letters (Romans 1:1-5, 16-17; 2:16; 10:16; 1 Corinthians 1:17; 2 Corinthians 4:4; Galatians 1:6-17; 3:8; and so on). But nowhere else does he sound like he is defining it in such a formal way. The gospel, as Paul outlines it here (1 Corinthians **15:3-8**), is what he preached and what the Corinthians received. It saves (**v 2**). It is traditional, in the best sense: Paul received it and passed it on faithfully as of "first importance" (**v 3**). Paul's first three verses sound like a drum roll, preparing us for the definition to follow. It sounds like we are about to hear a creed, and in many ways we are.

Before we get there, however, Paul makes an interesting aside, in which he qualifies the fact that the gospel has saving power: "… if you hold firmly to the word I preached to you. Otherwise, you have believed in vain" (**v 2**). This is the sort of thing you only say if you suspect some people are not holding firmly to the word—perhaps they are tampering with it in some way or even denying it—and are therefore at risk of believing in vain. Exactly why Paul says this will have to wait until the next section. But given the definition he is about to provide, we can assume it has something to do with resurrection.

The Gospel in Miniature

So here is the gospel in miniature: "… that Christ died for our sins according to the Scriptures, that he was buried, that he was raised on the third day according to the Scriptures, and that he appeared…" (**v 3-5**). This is one of the most important sentences ever written. It is hugely important theologically in that it defines the essence of the Christian message: the death of Jesus Christ for our sins, his burial, his resurrection from the dead on the third day and his appearances to many, all to fulfil the promises of Scripture. It describes Jesus as the *Christos*: the Christ, the Messiah, the King of Israel. It describes his death in substitutionary and biblical terms—"for our sins according to the Scriptures"—laying the foundation for all subsequent **atonement** theology. It includes the burial of Jesus as an element of Christian proclamation, which seems a surprising move until you meet someone who believes that Jesus didn't really die on the cross (like a Muslim) or that his body was eaten by wild animals (like the occasional university professor). And it details the many, many witnesses to his resurrection from the dead—the significance of which will be drawn out as this chapter continues—including Cephas (Peter), the Twelve, 500 other people, James the Lord's brother, all the apostles and finally Paul himself (**v 5-8**).

It is equally important historically. It is the earliest such definition we have, dating to the early 50s AD, and referring back to a set of beliefs that are even earlier. (The traditional form of words indicates that the crucifixion, burial, resurrection and appearances had been verbally packaged this way for some time.) This matters enormously. It means that despite the conspiracy-promoting paperbacks and op-eds that get published every Easter, the Christian belief in Jesus' death for our sins and his resurrection from the dead go back to the 40s at the very latest, and probably the 30s. It also means that the witnesses to the resurrection appearances were mostly still alive at the time of writing (**v 6**). As many have pointed out since, this makes it extremely unlikely that the stories are fabricated and provides powerful support for the belief that the resurrection of Jesus actually happened.

So does Paul's own testimony. He saw the risen Christ himself on the road to Damascus, although because it was after the ascension, and a while after the other apostles saw Christ, he regards himself as "one abnormally born" (**v 8**). He goes further: he is not just the last eyewitness but the "least of the apostles", hardly deserving the name of apostle because of his persecution of God's church (**v 9**). This is not false humility on Paul's part. He recognises that his encounter with the resurrected Jesus was far later, and his life to that point far worse, than those of the other apostles. But he will not wallow in self-pity about it or underplay his apostolic authority to proclaim

> Here is a momentous passage— arguably the weightiest in the entire New Testament.

the gospel, because the grace of God transformed him (**v 10**). As a result, it doesn't really matter whether the Corinthians (or any other first-century Christian) heard the message from Paul or from one of the other apostles, because they all preached the same gospel (**v 11**).

It is a momentous passage—arguably the weightiest in the entire New Testament. Yet we are still not done. As he concludes his summary of the gospel, Paul cannot help but point the Corinthians back to the grace of God at work in his own life. Paul is often seen as the apostle of the grace of God, partly because of the dramatic transformation it brought about in his own life, and here he exults in that with a rich and famously paradoxical statement: "But by the grace of God I am what I am, and his grace to me was not without effect. No, I worked harder than all of them—yet not I, but the grace of God that was with me" (**v 10**).

It is grace—the unmerited, transforming favour of God—which came to Paul when he was persecuting the church and turned him into the person he was as he wrote this letter. Grace changed him beyond recognition; it was, with delightful understatement, "not without effect". But it did not change Paul by acting upon him from the outside, with him as a passive recipient; it changed him by transforming him from within, with him as an active participant who, in response to grace, "worked harder than all of them". Yet even as Paul was working harder than anyone, as we saw most notably in chapter 9, the hard work was itself the result of "the grace of God that was with me" rather than Paul's own capacity. To use technical language for a moment, this is not synergism (we work alongside God), or even monergism (God does all the work, and we don't), but what theologian John Barclay calls energism (God works within us by transforming our **agency**). Or, in simpler terms, grace works.

How Can You Say That?

Until the start of this chapter, this letter has been a series of responses to issues or questions arising in Corinth, whether prompted by things Paul has heard (chapters 1 – 6) or by things the Corinthians have written (chapters 7 – 14). So far, Paul has always stated the subject up front: *I hear that there are divisions among you! A man has his father's wife! Now, about idol food…* and so on.

This chapter is different. If we were reading it for the first time, we would probably be wondering by now what it was all about; besides a cryptic hint in **15:2**, we would have no idea why Paul was summarising the gospel in this way. Finally, it becomes clear: "But if it is preached that Christ has been raised from the dead, how can some of you say that there is no resurrection of the dead?" (**v 12**). Some people in the church—and we cannot be sure how many but enough to warrant writing to them about it—have decided that they no longer hold to the future resurrection of believers. The resurrection of Jesus might be fine as a one-off, they reason. The immortality of the soul, widespread in Greek culture from the **classical period** onwards, is no problem either. But the idea that all our bodies will come out of the grave, raised indestructible and destined to live for ever, is a bridge too far. *It is embarrassing, implausible, Jewish, and it doesn't really matter that much,* they appear to have argued. *Let's drop it.*

Paul is aghast. If you lose the resurrection of the dead, you lose the resurrection of Christ as well (**v 13**)—and the resurrection of Christ is the be-all and end-all of Christian preaching (**v 1-11**). So if Christ is still dead, then both Paul's preaching and the Corinthians' faith are completely useless (**v 14**); they might as well all pack up and go home. Christianity is nothing without the risen Christ. Not only that, but witnessing to the resurrection (as Paul himself continually does, along with the other apostles) has made them all liars, because they have based their proclamation on a falsehood (**v 15**). If the dead are not raised, then Christ hasn't been raised either (**v 16**), and that means that the Christian faith is pointless, sins have not been forgiven (**v 17**), those who have died are lost for ever (**v 18**), and Christians are the most pitiful people on the face of the earth (**v 19**). The stakes could not be higher.

Paul's argument is both rhetorically powerful and painstakingly logical. Its logic probably appears obvious to us, in a world where people either accept both Christ's resurrection and ours or reject both, but are very unlikely to believe in one and not the other. But it was clearly not so obvious in Corinth. So Paul lays it out in an emphatic sequence, showing all the consequences that follow if you do not (as the **Nicene Creed** would later put it) "look for the resurrection of the body, and the life of the world to come". *That doctrinal misstep might seem trivial to you,* Paul says, *but if you take it you end up with a faith that is empty, futile, false, hopeless and pitiful. Abandon that, and you lose the farm.*

This Would Make Christianity Crash Down

It is no surprise to hear that the resurrection is important. What is fascinating, however, is just how much would unravel for Paul if the resurrection of Jesus were not true. If the corpse of Jesus had been found somewhere in the Middle East, it would not just mean that the walls of Christianity needed repointing; it would mean the entire house had come crashing down. If Jesus is still dead, then sins have not been forgiven. If Jesus is still dead, then we are all lost, hopeless liars. If Jesus is still dead, then our lives are not just mistaken, but "we are of all people most to be pitied" (**v 19**). The gospel cannot survive a dead Saviour.

The American pastor John Piper tells the story of a monk who was asked how he would feel if it turned out that Christianity was not true (in "Suffering and the Glory of God", preached at the Passion Conference in January 2006). Would this monk feel that he had wasted his life? The monk considered the question, and then responded. "Holiness, silence and sacrifice are beautiful in themselves," he replied, "even without promise of reward. I still would have used my life well." It sounds like a lovely sentiment. But Piper goes on to point out how different this is from what Paul says here. For Paul, it would mean his life had not just been wasted but had been more pitiful than anyone else's. Everything hangs on whether Christ came out of the tomb, and if he didn't, then we should all do something else.

"But Christ has indeed been raised from the dead" (**v 20**).

Questions for reflection

1. Does this passage prompt you to reshape the way you would communicate the gospel message to an interested non-Christian friend?

2. Is your attitude towards your work or ministry like Paul's in verse 10? In what areas do you need to pray for humility? In what areas do you long for God to work in you more?

3. What difference can the reality of the resurrection make in your life today?

PART TWO

The Death of Death

In the first part of chapter 15, Paul established two vital truths: that Jesus has risen from the dead (v 1-11), and that if he hasn't, and if therefore you won't either, then Christianity is a complete waste of time (v 12-19). In this next paragraph he makes the same argument more positively and in a way that has brought hope to billions of grieving and suffering Christians for twenty centuries. Christ has indeed risen from the dead—praise God!—and because he has, you will too.

To make this point, Paul pictures Christ as "the firstfruits of those who have **fallen asleep**" (**v 20**). Firstfruits, as the name implies, were the first part of the crop (of wheat, olive oil, grapes or whatever) to emerge every year, and they were given as an offering to God—but they were also celebrated, because they served as a guarantee that the rest of the crop was coming. (I have a tree in my garden that works this way: it flowers early, and when it does, I know that the rest of the plants and trees will bloom and produce fruit shortly afterwards.) Christ's resurrection, Paul says, is like this. He is the offering set aside for God, the sanctified **firstborn** from among the dead, but he is also the guarantee that all his people will be resurrected as well. Because he has burst forth into life, you can know for certain that it is only a matter of time before all his people do too.

There is a **federal** logic at work here. All of us are united to a federal head, whether Adam (through our shared humanity) or Christ (through our faith in him). If we are in Adam, through whom death came, we will die; if we are in Christ, through whom resurrection came, we will be made alive (**v 21-22**). But everything happens in order. Christ rises first, as the firstfruits, and "then, when he comes, those who belong to him" (**v 23**). The present age is a period of waiting. Yet we do not wait with doubt and concern but with certainty and expectation. We wait for our own resurrection like a farmer who has gathered his firstfruits waits for the rest of the crop to come, or like someone who has seen a flash of lightning waits for the thunder to follow. Christ has been raised, which ensures that we will be as well.

"Then the end will come" (**v 24**). When all who belong to Christ have been raised from the dead, Jesus will finally "[hand] over the kingdom to God the Father after he has destroyed all dominion, authority and power". Waiting for our resurrection can be hard, especially in times of suffering, and Paul knows this better than anyone. But there is a reason for the delay. We are waiting not just for our own resurrection but for all dominions, authorities and powers that oppose the reign of Christ to be destroyed—demons, emperors, philosophies and idols—because "he must reign until he has put all his enemies under his feet" (**v 25**). As yet, this is not complete. But it is certain. And "the last enemy to be destroyed is death" (**v 26**).

In December 1941, when Winston Churchill first heard that the Japanese had bombed the American Pacific Fleet as it lay at anchor at Pearl Harbor, he wrote something in his diary that captures beautifully the spirit of what Paul says here. Churchill was confident that America would now enter the war against Germany as well as Japan, which would mean that the result was a foregone conclusion, even if it would take many years to come about (and of course he was right). He said this:

> "So we had won after all! ... We had won the war ... No doubt
> it would take a long time ... Many disasters, immeasurable cost
> and tribulation lay ahead, but there was no more doubt about
> the end ... Being saturated and satiated with emotion and
> sensation, I went to bed and slept the sleep of the saved and
> thankful." (Winston Churchill, *The Second World War*, 3:477)

Paul—and you and I—can be certain of our salvation, and our future victory over death, even though we are still waiting for all things to be put under Christ's feet. We can sleep the sleep of the saved and thankful.

In the final two verses of this section, to avoid misunderstanding, Paul clarifies what he means by "everything" being put under Christ's feet. "Everything", he explains, does not include God the Father. That should be obvious: God is the one who has put everything under Christ's feet, not one of the things that get put there (**v 27**). In fact, once the mopping-up operation is completed, the Son will be subject to the Father, not the other way around (**v 28**); Paul makes this point to address the possible confusion of his "subjection" language, not to imply that this is the first time that the Son has submitted to the Father. Ultimately, God will be all in all.

Two Additional Arguments

Verses 29-34 give another two reasons why it makes no sense for the Corinthians to abandon their belief in the future resurrection. The first seems a little bizarre; I remember that it was the first Bible passage I ever read that made me go to my pastor and demand an explanation. "Now if there is no resurrection, what will those do who are baptised for the dead? If the dead are not raised at all, why are people baptised for them?" (**v 29**). Wait: what? People should get baptised for the dead? My pastor responded, rightly, that Paul is not endorsing the practice of baptising people for the dead but rather taking something that the Corinthians are known to be doing and pointing out that it makes no sense if there is no resurrection. If the dead are not raised and bodies simply remain in the ground, then baptising people on their behalf is clearly ridiculous, which means the Corinthians are not even being consistent with their own practices. So no, my pastor explained, we should not baptise people on behalf of the dead—and nor should we abandon our hope in the future resurrection.

The second argument is more about Paul than the Corinthians: "Why do we endanger ourselves every hour?" (**v 30**). *I spend my life in danger,* he says, *constantly facing the threat of death and continually fighting battles against false teachers and pagan rulers who are trying to destroy the church.* (The "wild beasts in Ephesus" here are not literal animals, which Paul, as a Roman citizen, would not have been subjected to, but either false-teacher "wolves" trying to destroy the sheep—see Acts 20:29—or the "beasts" of pagan empire oppressing God's people—see Daniel 7:1-18—or perhaps both.) *But if the dead are not raised,* Paul continues, *why would I bother?* If there is no resurrection and all we have are "human hopes", then we should all just eat and drink because tomorrow we will be dead (1 Corinthians **15:31-32**).

He concludes with a more direct challenge, urging them (as he has before) not to be deceived: "Bad company corrupts good character" (**v 34**). This crisp phrase summarises much of what is going on at Corinth. Worldly habits, values and practices are entering the church—culturally, sexually, legally, liturgically and theologically—and even within the congregation "there are some who are ignorant of God", to the shame of the church. A little mould spreads through the cheese (5:6). Bad friends corrupt good characters. The Corinthians need to come back to their senses and stop sinning. As we have already seen, and as Paul will teach at more length in his next letter (2 Corinthians 6:14 – 7:1), that may mean separating from certain sorts of people. Better that than losing the hope of the resurrection!

The Resurrection Body

For many years I taught a theology and discipleship course for 18-25-year-olds. Every year I would teach on the future hope of believers, and every year the first question would be something like this: "What kind of body will we have in the resurrection?" My usual approach was to be a bit mischievous and quote directly from this passage, where the Corinthians ask that exact question and Paul gives a fairly robust response: "How foolish!" (1 Corinthians **15:35-36**). Probably, however, the Corinthians are not asking a good-faith question here. The tone of Paul's reply makes it likely that they are not enquiring genuinely, as my students were, but mocking the idea of the future resurrection as absurd: *What kind of idiot believes you can live forever in a body? Bodies age, and decay, and die, and eventually rot.*

So how on earth is that supposed to work? It is that sneering, snarky scepticism that Paul regards as foolish.

His fuller answer is intriguing: "What you sow does not come to life unless it dies. When you sow, you do not plant the body that will be, but just a seed" (**v 36-37**). They think it sounds crazy that God would give us resurrection bodies, which are both in continuity with the fragile bodies we have now and somehow different from them. But that is exactly what happens when we plant a seed. We put a bit of wheat in the ground, and in "dying" it produces new life. But although the wheat is formed from the seed, it looks quite different: it is tall and thin and golden and wavy, not small and hard and round. Oak trees look nothing like acorns. Butterflies look nothing like caterpillars. It happens all the time. Bodies "die" and rise again to new life, and the new looks completely different.

> My future body is to my current body what an oak tree is to an acorn: identifiably the same, but greater to an unimaginable degree.

We can see it everywhere. There are all sorts of different "bodies" in creation—various kinds of seeds, animals, fish, birds, and even the sun, moon and stars—and all of them are created by God, and all of them are glorious in different ways (**v 38-41**). Given that variety, and the mysterious blend of continuity and discontinuity that exists between a seed and a plant, a resurrection body should be no problem at all. We see similar things around us every day.

"So will it be with the resurrection of the dead" (**v 42**). My future body is to my current body what an oak tree is to an acorn: identifiably the same, and with the life of the new emerging from the corpse of the old, but at the same time greater to an unimaginable degree. (I mean "unimaginable" quite literally: there is no way you could look at an acorn and imagine what an oak tree was like unless you had previously seen one, and it will be the same with the resurrection.) My current body is perishable, dishonourable, weak, and natural. I age. I decay overnight, and have to shower and wash and brush my teeth to keep my body presentable. My bones break if I fall badly. When I play football without stretching, my body aches. There are all kinds of things my body does not do that I wish it did (teleporting or flying, for instance), and a few things it does that I wish it didn't. In all manner of ways, my current body bears the image of Adam and reflects the realities of a world shrouded in death (**v 42-45**).

But the day is coming when it will be thoroughly transformed. When Jesus returns, death and all its sidekicks will be thrown into the trash for ever, and my body will reflect the realities of a world pulsing with resurrection life. It will be raised imperishable: unbreakable, impervious to disease, indestructible by sickness or the ravages of time (**v 42**). It will be raised in glory and power, free from the limitations and weaknesses of our present existence (**v 43**). It will no longer be modelled on the natural body of the first Adam, the soul-man who was given life and comes from dust; it will be modelled on the spiritual body of the last Adam, the spirit-man who gives life and comes from heaven (**v 45-48**). "Just as we have borne the image of the earthly man, so shall we bear the image of the heavenly man" (**v 49**). And when I consider the resurrection body of Jesus—his transformed physicality, whereby he could appear in a locked room and would never die, but could still hug his friends and enjoy a barbecue on the beach—I start to get quite excited about that. Teleporting looks a distinct possibility. Perhaps even flying is not off the table.

This is not wishful thinking (except in that I wish Christians would think about it more). For Paul, it boils down to a simple idea: what has happened to Jesus will happen to us. If Jesus defeated death and we are in him, then so will we. If Jesus' body has been transformed from weakness to power, so will ours be. If Jesus' experience of physicality has changed from dishonour to glory, from natural to spiritual, so will ours. If he left the grave behind him, so will I, and so will you.

Questions for reflection

1. Is it true of you that the way you live your life would make no sense without the future resurrection?

2. How does this passage make you more excited about our eternal future?

3. What is your greatest frustration with your current body? What hope does this passage give you?

12. A TRIUMPHANT ENDING

Sometimes the high point of Paul's letters comes in the middle. The richest theology and most soaring rhetoric in Romans, for instance, comes exactly halfway through its sixteen chapters, at the climax of chapter 8. The same is true of the equivalent sections in Galatians (3:26 – 4:7), Ephesians (3:14-21) and 1 Timothy (3:14-16), each of which stands in the centre of its letter like a dominant summit at the heart of a mountain range. Sometimes Paul peaks earlier, as he does in 2 Corinthians (5:12-21), Philippians (2:5-11) and Colossians (1:15-20).

Only in 1 Corinthians does Paul do what a novelist or screenwriter would, and reach his theological and rhetorical height near the end. (On several occasions I have "performed" Paul's letters in a conference setting, with an improvised paraphrase and lots of physical acting. The most dramatic and exhausting part of Romans comes at the midpoint, but the dramatic climax of 1 Corinthians is undoubtedly this section here.) You just have to read it to see why.

The Victory of God

The first line of **15:50** is open to misunderstanding: "I declare to you, brothers and sisters, that flesh and blood cannot inherit the kingdom of God". If we were not careful, we might conclude that Paul is teaching that the kingdom of God is not physical. We might imagine that his kingdom is a realm without bodies or matter or stuff—a **Gnostic** spirit-world where our souls float around in the clouds in heaven, as it is in much popular imagination and even a number of Christian hymns (I'm looking at you, "Away in a Manger"). As we should know by now, given the argument of the chapter so far, that is not what Paul means at all. When he says that flesh and blood cannot inherit the kingdom, he is not denying that the kingdom is physical, but rather he is denying that it is fleshly. The world to come is not made up of the kind of physicality—prone to corruption, decline and decay—that characterises our current sin-infested, death-marked world, and there-fore sin-infested, death-marked bodies will not enter it. We know this is what Paul means from the parallel phrase in the second half of the sentence: "… nor does the perishable inherit the imperishable". With-out being transformed in a bodily resurrection, we could not exist in the new world God is making (a point C.S. Lewis makes superbly in chapter 13 of *The Great Divorce*). Lightweight bodies of death do not belong in a heavyweight world of life.

This raises the obvious question: so how on earth (literally) will we inherit the kingdom? Paul's response sounds almost conspiratorial: "Listen, I tell you a mystery: we will not all sleep, but we will all be changed—in a flash, in the twinkling of an eye, at the last trumpet" (**v 51-52**). Not all Christians will die before Christ returns. Some of us will still be alive. But all of us, whether alive or dead, will be instan-taneously transformed when the last trumpet sounds. In an instant we will be raised imperishable, changed for ever and clothed with immortality (**v 53**).

It is worth reflecting for a moment on the two very ordinary images that Paul uses here: sleeping and clothing. The early Christians often spoke about death as "falling asleep". It was a euphemism, just as people today talk about "passing away". Their habit is far more bibli-cal and hope-filled than ours, however; the image of sleeping points forward to a day when we will wake up and rise, bodies and all, rather than vaguely "passing away" into an ethereal land of shadows. That's why Jesus used the image of sleeping (Mark 5:39; John 11:11-14), and it's why the apostles did too. That might be worth considering next time you attend a funeral.

The clothing image is another Pauline favourite, especially when it comes to the resurrection. It is a hugely insightful illustration. Our future resurrection is like trading a set of perishable, moth-eaten, mouldy clothes for a brand new outfit that will never perish or degrade: "The perishable must clothe itself with the imperishable, and the mortal with immortality" (1 Corinthians **15:53**). And that means that when we take these flesh-and-blood clothes off in death, we are not doing it in order to walk around naked for ever (without a body), but in order that we might put on incorruptible clothes that last for ever (with a resurrection body). Paul will make exactly this point in more detail in 2 Corinthians 5:1-5.

> Death—the mouth that swallows everything and is never satisfied—will itself be swallowed up in victory.

When that finally happens, then the words of the prophet Isaiah will be fulfilled at last: "Death has been swallowed up in victory" (1 Corinthians **15:54**; see Isaiah 25:8). It is only when every believer in history has put on a new body, immortal and imperishable, that Isaiah's words will finally come true. Isaiah was looking forward to a day in the future when death—the mouth that swallows everything and is never satisfied—would itself be swallowed up in victory. He drew in all kinds of images to show how glorious it would be: the establishment of a city of refuge, the overthrow of the ruthless, a massive banquet in which all the nations of the earth will eat Argentine beef and fine French wine, the wiping away of all tears, the removal of all shame, and the song of salvation (Isaiah 25:1-12). And Paul is saying that when the last trumpet sounds and the dead are raised, that saying will come to pass. So, Paul asks rhetorically, "Where, O death, is your victory? Where, O death, is your sting?" (1 Corinthians **15:55**). It sounds like a taunt at a football match. As one of my students put it once, "You're not stinging any more!"

Paul has taken this taunt from Hosea 13:14 and immediately points out the connection between the three key themes of death, sting and victory: "The sting of death is sin, and the power of sin is the law. But thanks be to God! He gives us the victory through our Lord Jesus Christ" (1 Corinthians **15:56-57**). Death is pictured as the insect—the bumblebee or wasp or whatever—while sin is the sting. We might expect it to be the other way around. Surely death is the wages of sin (Romans 6:23), not the other way around? But for Paul, it works both ways. Sin results from spiritual death (Romans 5), just as death results from sin (Romans 6), which in turn gets its power from the law (Romans 7). The only way the ultimate vicious cycle can be broken is through the victory of God, fulfilling the law and destroying both sin and death at once—which, in the Lord Jesus Christ, is exactly what has happened. Thanks be to God!

As he concludes the chapter, Paul brings a reassuring note of encouragement that links back to the way he started it. Without hope in the resurrection, there was always the possibility that the Corinthians had "believed in vain" (1 Corinthians 15:2), and that both Paul's preaching and their faith had been *kenos*: "useless" (v 14). But now he is confident that their work in the Lord is emphatically not *kenos* (translated "in vain" here in **verse 58**, but it is the same word). Christ has been raised, and we will be too, which means that no "labour in the Lord" is useless, and no work done in faith is in vain. Diligence has eternal consequences. Work—not just Christian ministry but ordinary, everyday labour in an office or on a construction site or in the home—is made meaningful by the fact that we, and everyone we work with (and for), will outlive this world. The effects of our parenting last for ever. So the Corinthians can stand firm, and let nothing move them, and always give themselves fully to what the Lord is doing in the world. The resurrection changes everything.

Generous Giving: Four Principles

Here's a question. Given all that we know about the Corinthians, and their corporate worship in particular, what would you regard as the essential elements of a biblical church service? What features of Christian liturgy ought to be included, come what may? Singing? Communion? Preaching? Prayer? Spiritual Gifts? Notices? Other?

Here is how the Heidelberg Catechism answered that question four and a half centuries ago (I've added the numbers for clarity):

"I regularly attend the assembly of God's people (i) to learn what God's word teaches, (ii) to participate in the sacraments, (iii) to pray to God publicly, and (iv) to bring Christian offerings for the poor."

It's a thought-provoking answer. It doesn't mean that other elements are unimportant or should not be included (and of course it is a catechism, not Scripture, so it is not our final authority anyway). But it is significant that when Reformation churches were trying to define the bare bones of a Christian service—in a society where people had far less money and possessions than we do now—they included giving to the poor alongside prayer, the sacraments and the proclamation of God's word. It would be interesting to know how many contemporary churches would agree.

Paul would: "Now about the collection for the Lord's people: do what I told the Galatian churches to do. On the first day of every week, each one of you should set aside a sum of money in keeping with your income, saving it up, so that when I come no collections will have to be made" (**16:1-2**). On the first day of the week (Sunday, the Lord's Day, Resurrection Day, or whatever we call it), Christians are not only to gather with other believers but we are also to set aside money for the care of the poor. In this case, the collection was specifically for the poor in Jerusalem, and would be taken there by specific individuals whose trustworthiness was not in question (**v 3**), possibly including Paul himself (**v 4**). But this was not a one-off. Paul had already told the Galatian churches to do the same thing (**v 1**), and his letters are filled with similar references, so much so that we can be confident that it was standard practice in his churches (Romans 15:23-33; 2 Corinthians 8 – 9; Galatians 2:10; Philippians 4:10-19; 1 Timothy 5:3-16; 6:17-19; see also Acts 24:17). It should be in ours, too.

Paul does not just urge generosity, however. He also teaches us how to give, with at least four principles that can help us today. First, he shows the priority of giving. Giving is something you should do "on the first day of every week" (1 Corinthians **16:2**), reflecting the ancient Israelite traditions of giving the first tenth ("tithing") and offering the "firstfruits" of the crop. It is not an afterthought or a tip, whereby you give whatever loose change you have lying around in your pockets or whatever cash you still have at the end of the month. God comes first. We should give what is right, not what is left. For many of us, that will mean giving by standing order at the start of the month, rather than emptying the leftovers of our piggy bank into the offering bucket at the end of it.

Second, Paul teaches the possibility of giving. "Each one of you should set aside a sum of money." Giving is not just for the rich. It is not something we start to do when we have enormous abundance. In my experience, many poorer individuals (and churches) actually give a higher percentage of their income than many rich individuals (and churches), and that is a dynamic we see in the New Testament as well (for instance in 2 Corinthians 8:1-5). A pastor in Bangladesh told me recently that they train people to tithe using rice, by getting them to set aside a bit of their allocation each mealtime and then give a jar to the pastor's family on Sunday. Most Western Christians can afford to give a lot more than that. The amount of giving will vary, but the reality of giving should not.

Third, we see the proportionality of giving: "Set aside a sum of money in keeping with your income" (1 Corinthians **16:2**). The amount we give should be proportional to our wealth. Rich people can give more than poor people (and rich people, in Paul's terms, would include virtually everyone reading this book), just as those with larger houses can host more people and those with more time can serve more. Our stewardship of wealth, like that of all the gifts we are given, should be proportional to what we have. At the same time, in our church we regularly remind people that we give out of what we have, not what we don't have (or hope to have!) If our spending accounts for 99% of our income and leaves us very little to give away, then the solution is to reduce our spending, not to charge into debt and hang the consequences. We give in keeping with our income.

And fourth, Paul outlines the practicality of giving. *Set money aside on a Sunday. Save it up. Make sure that we don't need to have a whip-round when I arrive,* he says, *because that would be awkward and embarrassing.* In short: plan your giving. Like all the spiritual disciplines, it is very unlikely to happen by accident. So mature Christianity involves making provision in advance and making the necessary sacrifices, because we love God and love our neighbours. Paul will return to this theme at much more length in his next letter (2 Corinthians 8 – 9).

Questions for reflection

1. What do you most look forward to about the resurrection and why?

2. How will you live now in light of the resurrection—think particularly about the areas of work, ministry and money?

3. What steps will you take to apply Paul's principles about giving to your own bank account?

PART TWO

I remember the first theology lecture I attended at university. It was the start of a course on Paul and his letters, and the lecturer began by saying that he was one of those scholars who thought Romans 16 was just as important for understanding Paul as Romans 1. I was baffled. Romans 1 contained the heart of the gospel; Romans 16 was a list of names I couldn't place and places I couldn't name. How on earth could the latter be as important as the former? Was the lecturer trying to provoke us by saying deliberately ridiculous things?

Twenty years later I can see that he was right. The closing chapters of Paul's letters, and especially his two longest ones, give us a wealth of insight into the social, geographical and cultural world of his churches that we would never have otherwise. Without passages like this one, it would be far too easy to collapse the Corinthians' context into ours, whether out of ignorance or just laziness. These apparently random lists of travel plans and personal greetings remind us that although this letter was written for us, it was not written to us.

Making Plans

Paul is writing from Ephesus, on the west coast of what is now Turkey, in the period leading up to **Pentecost** (1 Corinthians **16:8**). Within the timeline that Luke provides us in Acts, this probably fits in the "a little longer" of Acts 19:21-22, which would mean this letter was written in the spring of either AD 54 or 55. Paul's plan is to stay in Ephesus for the moment (for two reasons that we will come back to in a moment) before heading north up the coast, crossing the Aegean Sea into Europe (probably leaving from Troas, near the entrance to the Dardanelles), taking the Egnatian Way to the west and visiting the churches in Macedonia that he established in Philippi, Thessalonika, Berea and so on (1 Corinthians **16:5**; see Acts 16 – 17). After that, he plans to swing south into Achaia and visit the Corinthians, possibly even staying for the winter (1 Corinthians **16:6**). Partly this is because he wants them to help him on his journey—Paul is quite unapologetic about asking for help in his missionary activities, as we also see in 2 Corinthians and Romans—and partly it is because he wants to "spend some time with you," rather than making "a passing visit" (1 Corinthians **16:7**). Paul wants genuine relationship, not a fly-by or a whistlestop tour. Travelling preachers, including me, should take note.

In reality, things didn't quite turn out that way. Figuring out the aftermath of this letter involves a bit of detective work, but what seems to have happened is something like this. While still in Ephesus, Paul sent Timothy to Corinth (**v 10**), who found the church in chaos. Paul made a short visit to try to sort things out, but matters escalated, and he quickly went back to Ephesus, later describing the visit as "painful" and following it up with a strongly worded (and now lost) letter sent via Titus (see 2 Corinthians 2:1-4). This time the Corinthians were more repentant (2 Corinthians 7:5-16). Delighted with their response, Paul made another adjustment to his itinerary and then wrote 2 Corinthians from Macedonia. Based on what he says in Romans 15:19, we also know that at some point in this period he continued west on the Egnatian Way from Macedonia and eventually reached the Adriatic coast, following it up through Illyricum (modern-day Croatia) before eventually heading to Corinth for a third time (2 Corinthians 12:14). Finally he sailed back to Jerusalem.

We know that the church was unsettled by all these changes (2 Corinthians 1:15-18). But notice how provisional Paul is in his plans in this section. "Perhaps" (1 Corinthians **16:6**); "I hope to ... if the Lord permits" (**v 7**). Paul has travelled enough, and followed the leading (and sometimes the obstructing—see Acts 16:6-10!) of the Spirit enough, to know that things do not always work out the way that we think they will. So he is happy to disclose his plans, as long as people know that God in his sovereignty may see fit to change them. We would do well to imitate him when we make our own plans for the future, as James 4:13-17 reminds us.

One other thing worth noting from this paragraph is the two-pronged rationale for Paul's decision to stay in Ephesus: "a great door for effective work has opened to me, and there are many who oppose me" (1 Corinthians **16:9**). The mission in Ephesus was full of opportunities for the gospel. It was not just a door that was open for work; it was a great door that was open for effective work. Yet alongside the possibilities came persecution. "There are many who oppose me", he says, and in the previous chapter he compared his Ephesian struggles to fighting wild beasts (15:32). We might expect cities and cultures to fall into one of two categories: those that are closed to the gospel altogether and filled with dangerous persecution, and those that are open to the gospel and safe as houses. Some do. But most mission fields combine elements of both, with the doors for gospel advance wide open, yet with threats and dangers everywhere. It is helpful to know that this has always been true—and that for Paul, the opportunities outweighed the opposition.

Greeting Friends

Another reason for reading the endings of Paul's letters carefully is that they display the warmth and genuineness of relationship that unites Paul and his ministry partners, and the churches they serve. Without the conclusions to these letters, we might wonder if the frequency of words like "beloved" and "brothers and sisters" was merely rhetorical, or whether the continued references to his prayers for the churches were a stylistic affectation (like people today might sign an email with "Blessings" without any intention of actually praying for God to bless someone). After all, many Christians—and even Christian pastors—belong to denominations for years, even fundraising and church planting together, without seeming to enjoy the company and friendship of their "partners in the gospel". A friend told me how a pastor from another denomination approached him at a conference and said that he had been struck by the way my friend and his ministry partners clearly loved being together and laughing together, even to the point of having breakfast together. There are plenty of councils, committees, **presbyteries** and **synods** where people work with each other but don't seem to like each other very much. Might not Paul be the same?

The next few verses show otherwise. Paul's affection and love for the people of God, whether they are itinerant gospel preachers (Timothy, Apollos) or members of the Corinthian church (Stephanas, Fortunatus, Achaicus), is both undeniable and beautiful. With Timothy, Paul has a fatherly concern that the younger man not be fearful or dismissed by the Corinthians, "for he is carrying on the work of the Lord just as I am" (**16:10**). This overlaps closely with what we know from Paul's letters to Timothy, in which he is continually exhorting him to stand strong and not let others intimidate him or push him around (1 Timothy 1:18-20; 4:11-14; 5:19-21; 2 Timothy 1:6-8; 2:1-7; 4:1-5). Many of us will find it encouraging that God not only uses people like Paul—confident, assertive, bold, robust—but also uses people like Timothy, who seem more sensitive, gentle and harmonious. Paul's desire that the Corinthians "send [Timothy] on his way in peace" (1 Corinthians **16:11**) reflects this personal concern, as well as a desire that the letter that Paul is now writing, and that Timothy is carrying, be well-received.

The comments about Apollos could hardly be more different. Whereas Timothy is coming to Corinth at Paul's request (4:17), Apollos is not coming to Corinth, in spite of the fact that both Paul and the Corinthians want him to. It seems that the church had even written to Paul—the giveaway is the phrase "now about", which appears here for the sixth and last time (**16:12**)—asking him if he could encourage Apollos to come. So Paul tried. In fact, he "strongly urged him". But Apollos, perhaps upset by the way his name had been used in the factional arguments we read about in chapters 1 – 4, "was quite unwilling to go now, but he will go when he has the opportunity". We need to be careful about psychoanalysing people about whom we have very little information, but it certainly looks as if Timothy and Apollos (not to mention Barnabas, about whom we heard in chapter 9) are strikingly different characters, and thus Paul treats them very differently. Yet he clearly loves and values both of them.

Somewhat unexpectedly, Paul then gives a **staccato** list of five instructions that should characterise the Corinthians' behaviour: "Be on your guard; stand firm in the faith; be courageous; be strong. Do everything in love" (**16:13-14**). The first four of these are fairly typical for men in the Greco-Roman world; you can imagine the Roman General Maximus saying them to his men at the start of *Gladiator*. They remind us that, for Paul, the Christian life is a battle, filled with dangers and requiring constant vigilance against the world, the flesh and the devil. But the fifth one—which you would not have heard in this context from Maximus, or Plato or Aristotle or Cicero or Seneca or any other ancient pagan—reminds us what a radically Christian thinker Paul is. In many ways it is the summary not just of chapter 13 but of this entire letter, and in fact Christian ethics as a whole: "Do everything in love". The first four without the fifth will lead to disaster, and sadly we do not have to look too hard, even within the church, to find recent examples.

> Few things edify a church more than long-standing, devoted, refreshing leaders who are always among their people.

Finally Paul commends the household of Stephanas, who (presumably) had carried the Corinthians' letter to him. (We cannot prove it, but it seems likely that Fortunatus and Achaicus were members of Stephanas's household, whether slaves or adult sons.) Encouragement is always better when it is specific, and Paul identifies four particular ways in which they stand out. One: They were the "first converts"—or more literally the "firstfruits"—of Paul's ministry in Achaia, and a sign of future harvests to come. Two: "They have devoted themselves to the service of the Lord's people" (**16:15**). Three: "They have supplied what was lacking from you" (**v 17**), a phrase which sounds a bit backhanded in English but probably means something like "they made up for your absence" rather than anything pointed. Four: "They refreshed my spirit and yours also" (**v 18**), by bringing letters and greetings, and furthering friendship between the church and their apostle. Few things edify a church more than long-standing, devoted, refreshing leaders who are always among their people. As such, the Corinthians should submit to them, and to everyone who joins them in the work of the gospel (**v 16**), and honour them with recognition (**v 18**). Again, the depth of Paul's relationship with these individuals, and with the church as a whole, shines through.

Faith, Hope and Love

Churches do not just have relationships with other people; we have relationships with other churches. This is one of the most important conclusions we can draw from the way Paul ends his letters, and especially this one. The churches in the province of Asia—modern-day Turkey, where Paul is currently writing from—send greetings (**v 19**). So do Aquila and Priscilla, who are now in Ephesus with Paul but used to be members of the Corinthian church (Acts 18:1-4, 18-19), and so greet them "warmly in the Lord." So does "the church that meets at their house" (1 Corinthians **16:19**), as do "all the brothers and sisters here" in Ephesus. The picture is of a church that is much loved, not only by people who established it (like Paul) or who used to belong to it (like Aquila and Priscilla) but by hundreds of believers who have never been to Corinth and never will. One of the great benefits of Paul's model of apostolic ministry is the way it strengthens the interconnectedness and mutual love of the body of Christ across the world, not just from individual to individual but from church to church.

That said, there is no substitute for the physical presence of a local gathering. (I am writing these words during the covid-19 lockdown of 2020, which has shown once again how true this is.) So although the Corinthians are part of a much wider family of churches, all of whom send greetings, they have a unique responsibility in greeting one another, personally and physically, "with a holy kiss" (**v 20**). Paul even takes the pen himself at this point, rather than dictating it to Sosthenes (1:1), so that he can write a greeting in his own handwriting (**16:21**). In our digital world of video conferences and circular emails, it is helpful to be reminded of how important it is to interact with people and not just pixels, and how much affection can be communicated through handshakes and hugs and handwritten cards.

We are ready for the sign-off. But before finishing, Paul makes one last plea for the church to continue in faith, cling to hope and love the Lord (**v 22**). In an intense shot of Pauline theology, he proclaims both an **anathema** ("If anyone does not love the Lord, let that person be cursed!") and a *Marana tha* ("Come, Lord!") in a single verse. The two are connected. Paul felt free to do both, even amid a set of greetings and affirmations of love and grace; today, many (most?) churches do neither. The more we hope for the future return of Christ—and this is where Paul's letter both begins and ends—the more urgent the prospect of judgment will become and the richer our love for the Lord will be.

Paul ends with the two words that are the hallmark of his Christian life, and should be the hallmark of ours: grace and love. Ancient letters often concluded with a simple "farewell", just as we might sign off with "yours" or "all the best". But Paul always gives some variation on "the grace of the Lord Jesus be with you" (**v 23**); quite literally, his letters begin and end with grace. In this case, uniquely, he follows the grace with a reaffirmation of his love for all of them—maybe because he has spoken so forcefully to them, or because he is aware how vulnerable the relationship is, or simply because of the time he spent there and the depth of relationship they enjoy—before giving the Amen.

Questions for reflection

1. What can we learn from Paul's attitude towards his own plans?

2. How could you deepen your relationships with other Christians? How can you celebrate your unity and help each other to love Christ more?

3. As you come to the end of 1 Corinthians, how has the Spirit been changing you and challenging you? How has he been exciting you about what your church is, and what it could be?

GLOSSARY

Aaron: Moses' brother; the first priest to serve in the tabernacle.

Abraham: the ancestor of the nation of Israel, and the man God made a binding agreement (covenant) with. God promised to make his family into a great nation, give them a land, and bring blessing to all nations through one of his descendants (see Genesis 12:1-3).

Agency: our capacity to act or to do things.

Analogy: a comparison between two things, usually using one of them to explain or clarify the other.

Anathema: here, a curse.

Anthropology: the study of humans.

Apocryphal: legendary; a story about the past that is probably not true.

Apollos: an early Christian leader who preached in Ephesus and Corinth.

Apostasy: the abandonment of a religious belief or principle. An apostate is someone who once seemed to be a believer, but who later totally rejects Christ, turns away from sound teaching and leaves the church.

Apostles: the men who were appointed directly by the risen Christ to teach about him with authority.

Ascetic: refraining from fun and pleasure for religious reasons.

Atonement: a way of coming back into relationship with someone. In theology, Christ's death atones for our sin—enabling us to come back into relationship with God.

Blaspheme: to disrespect or mock God.

Calvary: the place on the outskirts of Jerusalem where Jesus was crucified.

Calvinistic: describes the teachings of John Calvin, a French theologian and pastor during the Reformation in the 16th century, based mainly in Geneva.

Canon: the collection of texts which are accepted as God's word.

Carnal: relating to the flesh or body.

Celibate: someone living a celibate life has decided not to enter into any sexual relationships.

Charismata: spiritual gifts (including wisdom, faith, gifts of healing, prophecy and tongues: see 1 Corinthians 12:1-11).

Charismatic: in charismatic churches, there is an emphasis on the experience and use of the gifts of the Holy Spirit listed in 1 Corinthians 12:8-10. By contrast, cessationist churches hold that these gifts are no longer experienced by Christians today.

Church discipline: the practice of reprimanding church members when they are perceived to have sinned, in the hope that the offender will repent and be reconciled to God and the church. It is also intended to protect other church members from the influence of sin.

Circumcision: cutting off the foreskin of a man or boy. God told the men among his people in the Old Testament to be circumcised as a way to show physically that they knew and trusted him, and belonged to the people of God (see Genesis 17).

Classical period: the name given to the cultures of the Mediterranean between the 5th century BC and the 4th century AD.

Commentary: a book that explains parts of the Bible verse by verse.

Commentator: the author of a commentary.

Communion: sharing bread and wine together to remember the death of Jesus.

Complementary: going well together.

Conservative: in conservative churches, there is not an expectation that the spiritual gifts listed in the New Testament (for example in 1 Corinthians 12:8-10) will be experienced and/or used when the church gathers. Usually, though not always, this is because they hold a cessationist position: that these gifts are no longer given by the Spirit today.

Covenant: a binding agreement or promise. The "old covenant" set out how believers in the Old Testament related to God; Jesus established the "new covenant", so believers now relate to God through his saving death and resurrection.

Cult: a religious community that exercises excessive and unhealthy power over its members.

David: the second king of Israel, whose reign was the high-point of Israel's history; the author of many psalms.

Denominations: different branches of the church, for instance Presbyterian, Southern Baptist, Anglican, Methodist.

Discipleship: being someone's disciple means learning from them and following their example.

Doctrine: a statement of a belief about God.

Ecstatic experience: an experience in which someone feels especially close to God, often in an overwhelming way.

Elders: men who are responsible for the teaching and ministry of a church.

Elijah: an Old Testament prophet who announced God's judgment for his people's idolatry.

Eschatology: an understanding of the "last times": death, judgment and eternity.

Ethical: to do with how one should behave.

Eucharist: the meal in which Christians share bread and wine to remember the body and blood of Jesus. Also called communion or the Lord's Supper.

Evangelical: emphasising the Bible's authority and the need to be personally converted through faith in Jesus' death and resurrection.

Exegetical: to do with exegesis, the practice of studying the words of the Bible and explaining what they mean.

Fall asleep: in this context, to die.

Federal: relating to a system whereby separate entities are controlled or ruled by a central power. For example, in the US political system, the federal government is the body that rules over all the states in the union.

Firstborn: the oldest child in a family; the first to be born.

Fundamentalist: believing in the strict, literal interpretation of Scripture.

Gentiles: people who are not ethnically Jewish.

Gnostic: follower of the teaching (prevalent in the first few centuries AD) that physical matter is evil and freedom comes from attaining special secret knowledge (or "gnosis").

Grace: undeserved favour. In the Bible, "grace" is usually used to describe how God treats his people. Because God is full of grace, he gives believers eternal life (Ephesians 2:4-8); he also gives them gifts to use to serve his people (Ephesians 4:7, 11-13).

Halal: meat prepared according to Muslim law.

High church: Christian churches which emphasise tradition and formality. High church services may feature choral music, the burning of incense, formal words and special robes.

Honour-shame culture: a culture in which standards of behaviour are based on how others will perceive us. There is a high emphasis on preserving one's honour and on not being publicly disgraced. This contrasts with a guilt culture, in which there is more emphasis on one's own conscience.

Infallible: not able to be incorrect.

Joseph: the second-youngest son of Jacob, and the great-grandson of Abraham.

Justification: the declaration that someone is not guilty, not condemned, completely innocent.

Legalism: a way of living that obeys certain rules in the belief that keeping these requirements will earn some form of blessing (for example, eternal life or worldly wealth).

Liturgy: set words used in some churches' services.

Lord's Supper: the meal in which Christians share bread and wine to remember the body and blood of Jesus. Also called communion or the Eucharist.

Lord's Table: another term for the Lord's Supper.

Lot: the nephew of Abraham.

Luther, Martin: a German theologian in the 16th century during the Reformation. His teachings (and those of his close followers) are described as **Lutheran.**

Majority world: the countries in which most of the world's population lives: that is, not in the richest nations. Sometimes called the developing world or third world.

Messiah: Christ, the anointed one. In the Old Testament, God promised that the Messiah would come to rescue and rule his people.

Metaphor: images which are used to explain something, but that are not to be taken literally (for instance, "The news was a dagger to his heart").

Midianite: a person from Midian, an area in the northwest Arabian Peninsula.

Moabite: a person from Moab, a region to the east of Judah.

Monogamy: the practice of only being married to one person at a time.

Monotheist: someone who believes in only one God.

Moses: the leader of God's people at the time when God brought them out of slavery in Egypt. God communicated his law (including the Ten Commandments) through Moses, and under Moses' leadership God guided them towards the land he had promised to give them. The first five books of the Bible are said to have been written by Moses.

Mystery: in Paul's writing, a mystery is something which is impossible to understand without God revealing it.

Nicene Creed: a statement of Christian belief written in the 4th century.

Parable: a memorable story told to illustrate a truth.

Passover: the event recorded in the book of Exodus, when God rescued his people from slavery in Egypt through sending plagues, the final one of which was the death of the firstborn in every family, which could be avoided only by killing a lamb in the firstborn's place so that God's judgment would "pass over" that household (see Exodus 12).

Patriarch: one of the "first fathers" of Israel, to whom God gave his promises—Abraham, Isaac and Jacob.

Pentateuch: the first five books of the Bible.

Pentecost: a Jewish feast which celebrates God giving his people his law on Mount Sinai (Exodus 19 – 31). On the day of this feast, 50 days after Jesus' resurrection, the Holy Spirit came to the first Christians (Acts 2), so "Pentecost" is how Christians tend to refer to this event.

Pentecostal: a Christian tradition which emphasises the Holy Spirit and the experience of the presence of God.

Phinehas: a priest in the time of Moses. See Numbers 25:6-13.

Polytheistic: believing in many gods.

Post-Christian: no longer characterized by Christian beliefs or morality.

Presbyterian: a Christian denomination with its roots in the Protestant Reformation.

Presbytery: the group of ministers and elders who govern Presbyterian churches within each district.

Priesthood: the system in the Old Testament whereby priests were responsible for representing the people to God.

Protestant Reformation: the religious revolution which took place in Western churches in the 16th and 17th centuries. Its leaders rejected some of the core beliefs of (what would become known as) Roman Catholicism, and sought to go back to what the Bible said, especially regarding how Jesus saves us and what the church is. The Reformation gave rise to the founding of Protestant denominations such as the Church of England, the Lutheran Church and the Presbyterian Church.

Providence: the protective care and power of God, who directs everything for the good of his people.

Purgatory: in Roman Catholic thought, the place where the souls of the dead are believed to go to be "purged" of their sin, before they are fit to enter heaven.

Redemption: the act of freeing or releasing someone; buying someone back for a price. This is what Jesus did for sinners: the price he paid was death on the cross.

Reformers: the leaders of the Protestant Reformation.

Renewal of all things: the future time when, after Jesus returns in judgment, the world will be made new.

Reverse psychology: the practice of subtly encouraging someone to do something by telling them to do the opposite thing.

Rhetorical: to do with speaking or expressing oneself well.

Sacrament: a rite or ceremony that symbolises a spiritual reality. In Protestantism, the Lord's Supper and baptism are considered sacraments.

Sacramental: in Protestant churches, the sacraments refer to baptism and the Lord's Supper.

Sanctification: the process of becoming more like Christ, by the work of the Holy Spirit.

Scribe: someone who writes or copies out documents.

Solomon: the king who succeeded David. He built the temple in Jerusalem and was renowned for his wisdom.

Soteriological: to do with being saved.

Spiritual gifts: God-given talents or abilities.

Staccato: in music, a series of sudden, detached sounds.

Substitutionary: in place of another.

Synod: a church council, in which leaders or members from across a denomination gather to discuss and decide matters of administration or doctrine.

Table fellowship: gathering to eat together.

Theological: focusing on God's perspective and the truth about him.

Tongue-speaking: the ability to speak in tongues is a spiritual gift discussed in 1 Corinthians 12 – 14.

Trinitarian: relating to the biblical doctrine of the Trinity—that the one God is three Persons, distinct from one another, each fully God, of the same "essence" (or "God-ness"). We usually call these three Persons Father, Son and Holy Spirit.

Typology: the study of types or symbols. When we say something in the Old Testament is a "type of Christ", we mean it points forward to Jesus.

Westminster Confession of Faith: a formal statement of belief, set out in 1646, to which Presbyterian churches subscribe in full and to which many other "Reformed" churches subscribe in large part.

Zeitgeist: the defining spirit or mood of a culture or period of history: the general ideas, beliefs and assumptions common in that time and place.

Zwinglian: describes the teachings of Ulrich Zwingli, a theologian and leader of the Reformation in Switzerland in the 16th century.

BIBLIOGRAPHY

Edward Adams, *The Earliest Christian Meeting Places: Almost Exclusively Houses?* (T&T Clark, 2013

Sam Allberry, *Seven Myths About Singleness* (Crossway, 2019)

Winston Churchill, *The Second World War* (Penguin Classics, 2005)

Roy Ciampa and Brian Rosner, *The First Letter to the Corinthians* (Eerdmans, 2010)

Gordon Fee, *The First Epistle to the Corinthians* (Eerdmans, 1987)

David Garland, *1 Corinthians* (Baker, 2003)

Kyle Harper, *From Shame to Sin: The Christian Transformation of Sexual Morality in Late Antiquity* (Harvard University Press, 2013)

Tom Holland, *Dominion: The Making of the Western Mind* (Little, Brown, 2019)

J.B. Lightfoot, *Notes on the Epistles of St. Paul* (Macmillan, 1895)

Lucy Peppiatt, *Women and Worship at Corinth: Paul's Rhetorical Arguments in 1 Corinthians* (Wipf and Stock, 2015)

Tom Schreiner *Spiritual Gifts: What They Are and Why They Matter* (B&H, 2018)

C.H. Spurgeon, *The Autobiography of Charles H. Spurgeon* (Curts & Jennings, 1898-1900),

Anthony Thiselton, *The First Epistle to the Corinthians* (Eerdmans, 2002)

Andrew Wilson, *God of All Things* (Zondervan, 2021)

More For You

1 Samuel For You

"As we read this gripping part of Israel's history, we see
Jesus Christ with fresh colour and texture. And we see
what it means for his people to follow him as King in an
age that worships personal freedom."

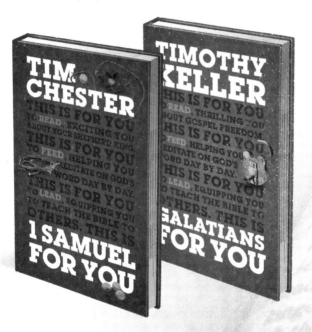

Galatians For You

"The book of Galatians is dynamite. It is an explosion of joy
and freedom which leaves us enjoying a deep significance,
security and satisfaction. Why? Because it brings us face
to face with the gospel—the A to Z of the Christian life."

God's Word For You Series

- **Exodus For You**
  Tim Chester

- **Judges For You**
  Timothy Keller

- **Ruth For You**
  Tony Merida

- **1 Samuel For You**
  Tim Chester

- **2 Samuel For You**
  Tim Chester

- **Psalms For You**
  Christopher Ash

- **Proverbs For You**
  Kathleen Nielson

- **Daniel For You**
  David Helm

- **Micah For You**
  Stephen Um

- **Luke 1-12 For You**
  Mike McKinley

- **Luke 12-24 For You**
  Mike McKinley

- **John 1-12 For You**
  Josh Moody

- **John 13-21 For You**
  Josh Moody

- **Acts 1-12 For You**
  Albert Mohler

- **Acts 13-28 For You**
  Albert Mohler

- **Romans 1-7 For You**
  Timothy Keller

- **Romans 8-16 For You**
  Timothy Keller

- **1 Corinthians For You**
  Andrew Wilson

- **2 Corinthians For You**
  Gary Millar

- **Galatians For You**
  Timothy Keller

- **Ephesians For You**
  Richard Coekin

- **Philippians For You**
  Steven Lawson

- **Colossians & Philemon For You**
  Mark Meynell

- **1 & 2 Timothy For You**
  Phillip Jensen

- **Titus For You**
  Tim Chester

- **Hebrews For You**
  Michael Kruger

- **James For You**
  Sam Allberry

- **1 Peter For You**
  Juan Sanchez

- **Revelation For You**
  Tim Chester

www.thegoodbook.com/for-you

COMPANY

BIBLICAL | RELEVANT | ACCESSIBLE

At The Good Book Company, we are dedicated to helping Christians and local churches grow. We believe that God's growth process always starts with hearing clearly what he has said to us through his timeless word—the Bible.

Ever since we opened our doors in 1991, we have been striving to produce Bible-based resources that bring glory to God. We have grown to become an international provider of user-friendly resources to the Christian community, with believers of all backgrounds and denominations using our books, Bible studies, devotionals, evangelistic resources, and DVD-based courses.

We want to equip ordinary Christians to live for Christ day by day, and churches to grow in their knowledge of God, their love for one another, and the effectiveness of their outreach.

Call us for a discussion of your needs or visit one of our local websites for more information on the resources and services we provide.

Your friends at The Good Book Company

thegoodbook.com | thegoodbook.co.uk
thegoodbook.com.au | thegoodbook.co.nz
thegoodbook.co.in